ADVANCE PRAISE FOR

Incorporation of the Bill of Rights

"In addition to specific amendments to the Constitution, the Supreme Court has a long history of incorporating certain rights and extending them to the states. In this careful and thoughtful study, Gary Bugh covers this development with clear and fascinating detail. A major contribution to our understanding of constitutional law and an important resource for scholars, attorneys, and judges."

—Louis Fisher, Visiting Scholar at the William and Mary Law School

"In this meticulously researched book, Professor Bugh individually examines each of the rights listed in the first eight amendments to the U.S. Constitution. He further indicates whether the Supreme Court has incorporated each right into the Due Process Clause of the Fourteenth Amendment and, if so, when it did. It is quite helpful and convenient to have this information assembled in a single place and with such attention to detail, including relevant case citations."

—John Vile, Dean and Professor of Political Science
at Middle Tennessee State University

"*Incorporation of the Bill of Rights* is the essential guide to which federal protections the U.S. Supreme Court has extended to the state level. Professor Gary Bugh provides an invaluable service with his detailed content analysis of justices' written opinions. The multiple essays of the book, each one covering a single right, offer a unique approach to understanding the topic, including the relationships between justices' theoretical defenses and incorporation rulings. Teachers, students, and legal professionals will find the book a reliable source about incorporation for years to come."

—Donald Gooch, Associate Professor of Political Science
at Stephen F. Austin State University

Incorporation of the Bill of Rights

This book is part of the Peter Lang Humanities list.
Every volume is peer reviewed and meets
the highest quality standards for content and production.

PETER LANG
New York • Berlin • Brussels • Lausanne • Oxford

Gary Bugh

Incorporation of the Bill of Rights

An Accounting of the Supreme Court's Extension of Federal Civil Liberties to the States

PETER LANG
New York • Berlin • Brussels • Lausanne • Oxford

Library of Congress Cataloging-in-Publication Control Number: 2022039014

Bibliographic information published by **Die Deutsche Nationalbibliothek.**
Die Deutsche Nationalbibliothek lists this publication in the "Deutsche Nationalbibliografie"; detailed bibliographic data are available on the Internet at http://dnb.d-nb.de/.

ISBN 978-1-4331-9631-7 (hardcover)
ISBN 978-1-4331-9632-4 (ebook pdf)
ISBN 978-1-4331-9633-1 (epub)
DOI 10.3726/b19589

Peter Lang Publishing, Inc., New York
80 Broad Street, 5th floor, New York, NY 10004
www.peterlang.com

Table of Contents

Acknowledgments

This volume of incorporated federal rights would not have been possible without the cooperation and assistance of several people. My family and friends have always supported my scholastic endeavors wherever they have taken me, which includes having civil discussions over complicated topics and issues. Texas A&M University extended support throughout the project. The blind reviewers and other scholars provided invaluable suggestions that enhanced my analysis. Guidance from the Peter Lang editors assured the production of a high-quality book. Overall, I am grateful to all those who think that it is a good idea to know about incorporation.

Preface

The vast literature on the U.S. Bill of Rights does not include many works identifying the federal civil liberties that the Supreme Court has protected against state violation. The Bill of Rights originally provided insulation from federal government abuse of power. Over time, mostly during the twentieth century, the Supreme Court selectively expanded these federal guarantees to the states. Some scholars and Court justices have identified incorporated rights and attending cases, but these lists do not correspond. Some scholars and justices include protections in their lists of incorporated rights that the Bill of Rights does not enumerate. Regardless, many of these and other works inspired me to investigate which Bill of Rights' protections the Court regards as incorporated.

Several pieces of scholarship that began to pique my interest in delineating incorporated rights included Fred Friendly and Martha Elliot's popular 1984 book, *The Constitution That Delicate Balance*, Paul Bartholomew's 1964 article in the *American Bar Association Journal*, "The Gitlow Doctrine Down to Date," Richard Cortner's 1981 *Second Bill of Rights book,* and Louis Fisher and Katy Harriger's regularly updated public law textbook, *American Constitutional Law.*

While incorporation was not the focus of Friendly and Elliot's book, they drew attention to why the Fourteenth Amendment and incorporated rights matter. The thrust of their narratives was that the Court's use of the Fourteenth Amendment Due Process Clause to protect rights against state transgression strengthened each person's ability to check government power. Bartholomew in a short article listed some incorporated rights and explained how *Gitlow v. New York* (1925) contributed to the Court's incorporation rationale. Cortner reviewed the Court's approaches to defending federal rights at the state level, described different incorporation timeframes, and identified several incorporation cases. Along with discussing political interests involved with Court rulings, Fisher and Harriger have provided one of the more detailed tables of incorporated rights and related cases. I am certainly indebted to these and other works addressing incorporation.

This book presents a catalog of incorporated rights and incorporation cases based on what justices have written in Court opinions. This does not mean that justices are right, or all agree about the incorporation standing of any given civil liberty. It also does not mean that the Court is necessarily the nation's defender of rights. In researching the Court's views on the incorporation status of federal civil liberties, I discovered a few surprises along the way. These included finding some rights that I thought the Court had already protected against states remain unincorporated, notably the due process guarantee of the Fifth Amendment and civil jury trial provisions of the Seventh Amendment.

This is a comprehensive study of the Court's incorporation of the Bill of Rights. Students, teachers, scholars, and practitioners will find this book an indispensable resource for understanding which federal civil liberties the Court has applied to the states and in which cases. It also illuminates incorporation as an important concept of America's political lexicon. This analysis is a step toward greater understanding of rights in civil society, suggesting new avenues of research, including finding additional Court confirmations of incorporated rights and evaluating the strength of civil liberties in the U.S. federal system.

Introduction

After decades of not doing so, the U.S. Supreme Court recently incorporated two federal rights: keep and bear arms of the Second Amendment and no excessive fines of the Eighth Amendment. The Bill of Rights addresses several civil liberties. Which ones has the Court protected against state governments? To find out, this work focuses on justices' written statements in their legal opinions about the extension of these rights to the state level. In other words, rather than scholars, commentators, or anyone else, which rights do justices regard as incorporated? Through an analysis of Court opinions, this volume also identifies the cases most relevant to incorporated and unincorporated rights.

This inventory of incorporated rights and attending cases provides a valuable resource for anyone interested in the nation's constitutional order. It serves as reminder of the importance of incorporation, which adds a layer of protection against government abuse throughout the United States. While states have their own constitutional rights, as the country's history demonstrates, local and state governments are more likely to suppress individual liberty if federal rights remain unincorporated. Incorporated rights strengthen individuals' power to control government. Yet, effective use of these civil liberties at the state level depends upon the continued support of the people, their representatives, and the Court. Gaining greater knowledge about incorporation enhances our understanding of rights.

Why Needed?

Along with a near absence of research distinguishing incorporated rights is an inconsistency among available lists. Occasionally, a justice in an opinion will identify incorporated rights along with related cases.[1] Some scholarship has addressed the incorporation status of a few Bill of Rights' protections.[2] Most constitutional law textbooks provide such tables. Discrepancies exist among all these listings, however.

Some simply leave aside a few rights, implying that the Court has not yet incorporated them, such as the First Amendment petitioning government guarantee.[3] It has not been uncommon for justices to cite different incorporation cases for the same right. For example, while many agree *Gitlow v. New York* (1925) incorporated the First Amendment right of free speech, some credit *Whitney v. California* (1927), *Fiske v. Kansas* (1927), *Lovell v. Griffin* (1938), *Staub v. Baxley* (1958), *Edwards v. South Carolina* (1963), *New York Times v. Sullivan* (1964), or some combination of these decisions.[4] Such is the case with some other rights. Not all justices recognize *Near v. Minnesota* (1931) as incorporating freedom of the press.[5] A few instead reference *Gitlow*, *Lovell*, *Grosjean v. American Press* (1936), *New York Times*, or two or more of these cases.[6] The general consensus is that the

1 For Supreme Court listings of incorporated rights along with relevant cases, see Justice Hugo Black in *Gideon v. Wainwright*, 372 U.S. 335, at 341–42 n. 4–7 (1963); Justice William Brennan in *Malloy v. Hogan*, 378 U.S. 1, at 4–6 n. 2, 4, 5 (1964); Justice Arthur Goldberg in *Pointer v. Texas*, 380 U.S. 400, at 412 n. 2–7 (1965) (concurring); Justice Bryon White in *Duncan v. Louisiana*, 391 U.S. 145, at 148–49 n. 4–12 (1968); and Justice Samuel Alito in *McDonald v. City of Chicago*, 561 U.S. 742, at 764–65 n. 12 (2010).

2 See, for example, Richard C. Cortner, *The Supreme Court and the Second Bill of Rights: The Fourteenth Amendment and the Nationalization of Civil Liberties* (Madison: University of Wisconsin Press, 1981); and Henry J. Abraham and Barbara A. Perry, *Freedom and the Court: Civil Rights and Liberties in the United States*, 8th ed. (Lawrence, KS: University Press of Kansas, 2003).

3 See, for example, *Duncan*, at 148 n. 5; and *McDonald*, 561 U.S. 742, at 764 n. 12.

4 See, for example, *Stromberg v. California*, 283 U.S. 359, at 368 (1931); *Gideon*, 372 U.S. 335, at 341 n. 4; and *Malloy*, 378 U.S. 1, at 5 n. 4. These cases variously reference *Gitlow v. People of New York*, 268 U.S. 652 (1925); *Whitney v. California*, 274 U.S. 357 (1927); *Fiske v. Kansas*, 274 U.S. 380 (1927); *Lovell v. City of Griffin*, 303 U.S. 444 (1938); *Staub v. City of Baxley*, 355 U.S. 313 (1958); *Edwards v. South Carolina*, 372 U.S. 229 (1963); and *New York Times Co. v. Sullivan*, 376 U.S. 254 (1964) for incorporating speech.

5 *Near v. State of Minnesota ex rel. Olson*, 283 U.S. 697 (1931).

6 See, for example, *Gideon*, 372 U.S. 335, at 341 n. 4; and *Malloy*, 378 U.S. 1, at 5 n. 4 (variously citing *Gitlow*, 268 U.S. 652; *Lovell*, 303 U.S. 444; *Grosjean v. American Press Co., Inc.*, 297 U.S. 233 (1936); and *New York Times*, 376 U.S. 254).

Court extended the Fourth Amendment protection against unreasonable searches and seizures to the states in *Wolf v. Colorado* (1949); however, some also include *Elkins v. United States* (1960) and *Mapp v. Ohio* (1961).[7]

One reason for the inconsistencies is that, in discussions about incorporation, justices tend to focus more on elaborating theoretical approaches than on identifying specific rights and cases. The Court in several decisions reasoned that the Due Process Clause of the Fourteenth Amendment protected a federal guarantee at the state level. Justices have often described this rationale along with cases in which the Court contributed to its development or used it to defend rights. For example, in his review of the Due Process Clause protection of "fundamental safeguards of liberty," Justice Hugo Black in *Gideon v. Wainwright* (1963) explained that the Court incorporated "speech and press" in *Gitlow* and *Lovell*, "speech" in *Staub*, and "speech, assembly, petition for redress of grievances" in *Edwards*.[8] Similarly, when Justice William Brennan in *Malloy v. Hogan* (1964) noted that the Court applied to the state level "speech and press" in *Gitlow*, *Lovell*, and *New York Times* and "speech" in *Staub*, he too was addressing the Court's use of the Due Process Clause to protect rights from state infringement.[9]

Another reason for differences among identified incorporation lists is that determining incorporated rights and their cases is no easy task. Along with referencing different or multiple cases for extending the same provision to the states, justices may disagree about the incorporation status of some rights. It may be that a lower federal court has protected a civil liberty against state governments, but the Court has not yet heard a case about the same right. Perhaps the Court perceives states as already following due process of law, negating a reason for extending a specific Bill of Rights' guarantee to the state level. It could be that the Court has held a right as a limitation only upon the federal government. It may have incorporated a single right in different cases to varying degrees.

Taking an Account

This review explores Court opinions to identify incorporated rights and relevant cases. The examined texts are numerous, beginning with justices' incorporation

7 See *Gideon*, 372 U.S. 335, at 342 n. 6; and *Malloy*, 378 U.S. 1, at 6 n. 5 (each crediting *Wolf v. Colorado*, 338 U.S. 25 (1949); *Elkins v. United States*, 364 U.S. 206 (1960); and *Mapp v. Ohio*, 367 U.S. 643 (1961)).

8 *Gideon*, 372 U.S. 335, at 341–42 n. 4.

9 *Malloy*, 378 U.S. 1, at 4–5 n. 4.

lists. Justice Samuel Alito's catalog of incorporated rights and corresponding cases in *McDonald v. Chicago* (2010) is more extensive than other justice descriptions but does not address every Bill of Rights' guarantee. Nevertheless, it serves as the starting point for selecting opinions to investigate for incorporation statements. Other justice compilations of incorporated federal guarantees offer additional suggestions while also confirming some of Alito's information. For civil liberties that justices did not mention in their incorporation listings, research consulted Court opinions that addressed the rights as well as scholarship to help identify cases to investigate. While analysis did not consider every judicial opinion, it investigated enough of those in the orbit of each federal right to answer whether the Court had extended the civil liberty to the states and in which case. This includes a gauge of the Court's confirmations of each incorporated right. References to "the Court" indicate at least plurality consensus, not necessarily that all justices agree on a right's incorporation defense, standing, or case.

In this content analysis of Court decisions, at least one statement asserting application of a Bill of Rights' protection to the state level in a majority or plurality opinion means that the Court has incorporated the right. Such incorporation statements may be apparent and distinct. However, some statements may be ambiguous or discursive, only clarified when considered in relation to the issue of the case, other passages in the opinion, statements in accompanying concurrences or dissents, or even other decisions. These initial statements also help identify the most relevant decision to a right's incorporation status.

Finding a clear confirmation statement in a subsequent decision from any kind of opinion, from majority to dissenting, lends supplemental support to a right's incorporation standing and case. This study does not try to identify all incorporation confirmations because doing so is not possible. While some of the Court's acknowledgments of an incorporated right may be obvious, others may be indistinct, such as mentioning a civil liberty in a broader context about rights at the state level. A justice may present a right as if the Court has incorporated it without providing further information. Justices may use different words or phrases to refer to the same right. The Court may view a right as so closely related to another one that it does not consistently distinguish between the two. As mentioned, it may credit more than one case for protecting a right against state violation. Nevertheless, this analysis provides approximate counts of incorporation confirmations.

Delving into what the Court regards as each right's incorporation status and case may offer insights into its most and least favored protections. Several clear Court confirmations of an incorporation case may indicate a favorite right whereas few such acknowledgments may suggest a vaguely incorporated one.

The primary sources of this analysis are the Court's published decisions in *U.S. Reports*.[10] The Library of Congress has publicly accessible scans of these original documents available online. The official Court opinions sometimes differ in minor ways from widely disseminated transcriptions found elsewhere on the internet. An effort was made to draw direct quotations from the original sources.

This work only considers enumerated rights of the first eight amendments. It does not investigate unenumerated protections that the Court has associated with the Bill of Rights, such as privacy and the exclusionary rule. While arguments could be made that the Ninth and Tenth Amendments—respectively protecting the people's rights and states' powers—encompass civil liberties, consideration of the first eight amendments follows the Court's conventional practice.[11] The first eight amendments present 29 distinct rights. This total includes "keep and bear Arms," "searches and seizures," and "jury of the State and district" as single rights each because that is how the courts have generally regarded them. For the text of the Bill of Rights, see Appendix A.

Approaching each enumerated right of the first eight amendments is done on an amendment-by-amendment, right-by-right basis. Reviewing rights in order of their corresponding amendments and arranged listings within each amendment provides the reader a manageable reference tool. Appendix B lists the incorporation status and case for each right in this original sequence. Each description of the Court's incorporation view of a right stands as its own essay, regardless of when the Court extended the protection to the state level. For example, the Court first incorporated religious exercise in 1940 and then the prohibition of government establishment of religion in 1947. However, because the First Amendment lists these rights in the reverse order, this review covers establishment before exercise.

Several of the essays describe the Court's theoretical defenses because these rationales were often integral to its application of rights to the state level. However, this book does not evaluate justices' arguments for and against incorporation. Doing so might involve close examination of premises and conclusions, as well as appeals to related concepts, such as fundamental rights, ordered liberty, scheme

10 Library of Congress, "United States Reports (Official Opinions of the U.S. Supreme Court)," *Digital Collections*. https://www.loc.gov/collections/united-states-reports/.

11 See, for example, *Grosjean*, 297 U.S. 233, at 243; *Palko v. Connecticut*, 302 U.S. 319, at 323, 326 n. 4 (1937); *Betts v. Brady*, 316 U.S. 455, at 462 (1942); *Adamson v. California*, 332 U.S. 46, at 67 (1947) (Frankfurter, F., concurring); *Poe v. Ullman*, 367 U.S. 497, at 515, 516 (1961) (Douglas, W., dissenting); *Malloy*, 378 U.S. 1, at 4 n. 2; 24 (Harlan, J., dissenting); and *Duncan*, at 148; 165 (Black, H., concurring).

of justice, and due process. Others have analyzed these incorporation defenses, although there is opportunity for more scholarship in this area.[12]

Each essay explores the judiciary's views of a Bill of Rights' protection before the incorporation decision. Reviewing earlier understandings of a federal guarantee is useful because justices often addressed these perspectives when protecting a right against states. With a focus on identifying which rights the Court regards as incorporated, this work does not offer a comprehensive review of each civil liberty from early America to post-incorporation consequences. The essays leave aside the impact that incorporated rights have had on practice, which can be found elsewhere.[13]

There is no quibble over the definition or use of the word "incorporation" in reference to the Bill of Rights. It conventionally means that the Court has extended a federal guarantee to the state level, protecting it from all governments throughout the United States. Incorporation also refers to the Court's view of a civil liberty as essential for due process of law and therefore the Due Process Clause of the Fourteenth Amendment includes the right. Some justices have occasionally used variants of incorporates, such as "absorbs," "applies," and "protects."[14]

The Court initially regarded the Fourteenth Amendment protection of due process of law at the state level as standing alone, with state constitutions and laws protecting specific rights. It then began to incorporate select Bill of Rights' guarantees into the Due Process Clause, first with just compensation in 1897, then with most First Amendment and a few other rights during the 1920s–1940s, and then fairly rapidly and succinctly throughout the 1960s with nearly all criminal trial protections. Appendix C chronologically lists incorporated rights and their respective cases.

12 See, for example, Louis Henkin, "Selective Incorporation in the Fourteenth Amendment," *Yale Law Journal* 73, no. 1 (November 1963), 74–88; Cortner, *Second Bill of Rights*; Jerold H. Israel, "Selective Incorporation: Revisited," *Georgetown Law Journal* 71, no. 2 (December 1982), 253–338; and Abraham and Perry, *Freedom and the Court*.

13 See, for example, Israel, "Selective Incorporation: Revisited"; Joshua Dressler and Alan C. Michaels, *Understanding Criminal Procedure: Volume 2, Adjudication*, 4th ed. (Durham, NC: Carolina Academic Press, 2015); Joshua Dressler, Alan C. Michaels, and Ric Simmons, *Understanding Criminal Procedure: Volume 1, Investigation*, 8th ed. (Durham, NC: Carolina Academic Press, 2021); Louis Fisher and Katy J. Harriger, *American Constitutional Law*, 12th ed. (Durham, NC: Carolina Academic Press, 2019); and Robert A. Carp, Kenneth L. Manning, and Lisa M. Holmes, *Judicial Process in America*, 12th ed. (Washington, DC: CQ Press, 2022).

14 See, for example, *Palko*, 302 U.S. 319, at 326; *Griswold v. Connecticut*, 381 U.S. 479, at 488 (1965) (Goldberg, A., concurring); and Felix Frankfurter, "Memorandum on 'Incorporation' of the Bill of Rights into the Due Process Clause of the Fourteenth Amendment," *Harvard Law Review* 78, no. 4 (February 1965), 746–83.

Since the *Malloy* ruling that states should protect incorporated rights "according to the same standards" as the federal government, which some justices criticized, the Court has made greater use of the word incorporation.[15] It should be mentioned that, despite the Court's adherence to the *Malloy* standard, states retain administrative discretion over many federal rights.[16] Regardless, the Court has since regularly used "incorporation" and referred to it in terms of bringing a federal right into the Due Process Clause, thereby protecting it from state transgression.[17] This book also makes use of the word.

Which Bill of Rights' protections has the Court incorporated? To find out, this accounting investigates justices' views about extending the enumerated rights of the first eight amendments to the state level. Each essay presents this content review for a right, other than the Conclusion, which summarizes the Court's incorporation of the Bill of Rights.

15 *Malloy*, 378 U.S. 1, at 10–11. See, for example, *Benton v. Maryland*, 395 U.S. 784, at 795 (1969); and *McDonald*, 561 U.S. 742, at 765–66.

16 William J. Brennan Jr., "The Bill of Rights and the States: The Revival of State Constitutions as Guardians of Individual Rights," *New York University Law Review* 6, no. 4 (October 1986), 535–53; and Fisher and Harriger, *American Constitutional Law*, 409.

17 See *McDonald*, 561 U.S. 742, at 763–66.

PART I

FIRST AMENDMENT

Establishment of Religion

"Congress shall make no law respecting an establishment of religion."

The Supreme Court in *Everson v. Board of Education* (1947) extended the Bill of Rights' prohibition against government establishment of religion to the states.[1] *Everson* completed the Court's incorporation of both First Amendment religious guarantees of exercise and establishment.

Before *Everson*

A few years prior to *Everson*, the Court incorporated the right to free exercise of religion in *Cantwell v. Connecticut* (1940).[2] It also argued in several cases that the Fourteenth Amendment due process of law protection of "liberty" included "fundamental rights." For example, Justice Owen Roberts in *Cantwell* held that the state law challenged by the appellants "deprives them of their liberty without due process of law in contravention of the Fourteenth Amendment."[3] The Court also

1 *Everson v. Board of Education of the Township of Ewing*, 330 U.S. 1 (1947).
2 *Cantwell v. Connecticut*, 310 U.S. 296 (1940).
3 Ibid., at 303.

used this Due Process Clause rationale to incorporate the First Amendment rights of speech in *Gitlow v. New York* (1925), press in *Near v. Minnesota* (1931), and assembly in *De Jonge v. Oregon* (1937).[4]

Without referencing these cases or the Due Process Clause specifically, Justice William Douglas in *Murdock v. Pennsylvania* (1943) asserted that the Fourteenth Amendment already protected the First Amendment rights of religion, speech, and press at the state level.[5] This is why for him, "[f]reedom of press, freedom of speech, freedom of religion are in a preferred position."[6] While not absolute, free religious exercise "exists apart from state authority. It is guaranteed the people by the Federal Constitution."[7] In his *Murdock* dissent, Justice Stanley Reed agreed with this view, referencing *Gitlow*, *Near*, and *Cantwell* when explaining that the Due Process Clause "is held to have drawn the contents of the First Amendment into the category of individual rights protected from state deprivation."[8]

While the Court used the due process defense to protect some civil liberties against state infringement, including religious exercise, it had not incorporated the prohibition against government establishment of religion. However, Roberts in *Cantwell* indicated that this was possible, arguing that the Fourteenth Amendment restrained state governments from violating both First Amendment religious rights.[9]

Everson v. Board of Education (1947)

In *Everson*, the Court extended the federal right against government establishment religion to the state level. This case regarded a state law that permitted school districts to reimburse parents for public bus fares to take their children to schools, which included private religious institutions.

Justice Hugo Black in the *Everson* opinion argued that the Fourteenth Amendment prohibited state governments from establishing religion. He referred to both religious guarantees throughout the opinion because he saw an "interrelation of these complementary clauses."[10] For example, he began by asserting

4 *Gitlow v. People of New York*, 268 U.S. 652, at 666 (1925); *Near v. State of Minnesota ex rel. Olson*, 283 U.S. 697, at 707 (1931); and *De Jonge v. Oregon*, 299 U.S. 353, at 364 (1937).

5 *Murdock v. Pennsylvania*, 319 U.S. 105, at 108 (1943).

6 Ibid., at 115.

7 Ibid.

8 Ibid., at 120–21; see also 126 n. 11 (Reed, S., dissenting; citing *Gitlow*, 268 U.S. 652, at 666; *Near*, 283 U.S. 697, at 707; and *Cantwell*, 310 U.S. 296, at 303).

9 *Cantwell*, 310 U.S. 296, at 303.

10 *Everson*, 330 U.S. 1, at 15.

that "[t]he First Amendment, as made applicable to the states by the Fourteenth, *Murdock v. Pennsylvania*, commands that a state 'shall make no law respecting an establishment of religion, or prohibiting the free exercise thereof.'"[11] Sharing the sentiment some justices expressed earlier, he regarded the Fourteenth Amendment as extending all First Amendment rights to the states.[12] However, "some states persisted for about half a century in imposing restraints upon the free exercise of religion and in discriminating against particular religious groups."[13] Black argued that "the Fourteenth Amendment was interpreted to make the prohibitions of the First applicable to state action abridging religious freedom," for which he noted several religion cases, leading with *Cantwell* and including *Murdock*.[14] Continuing, he held that "[t]here is every reason to give the same application and broad interpretation to the 'establishment of religion' clause."[15]

Black did not refer to the Due Process Clause, but the Fourteenth Amendment loomed large in his defense of the right against government establishment of religion at the state level. Using the language of the Fourteenth Amendment, he listed several examples of what "[t]he 'establishment of religion' clause of the First Amendment means," beginning with "[n]either a state nor the Federal Government can set up a church. Neither can pass laws which aid one religion, aid all religions, or prefer one religion over another," and ending with "[n]either a state nor the Federal Government can, openly or secretly, participate in the affairs of any religious organizations or groups and *vice versa*."[16] Therefore, "New Jersey cannot consistently with the 'establishment of religion' clause of the First Amendment contribute tax-raised funds to the support of an institution which teaches the tenets and faith of any church."[17] Appealing to Thomas Jefferson's view of keeping government and religion separate, Black concluded with "[t]he First Amendment has erected a wall between church and state. That wall must be kept high and impregnable. We could not approve the slightest breach."[18]

While the Court ruled in a close 5-4 vote that the state had not actually violated the constitutional protection against establishment of religion, Black took the opportunity to emphasize that the right applied at the state level. He elaborated that the First Amendment requires a state government to be "neutral in

11 Ibid., at 8 (citation information omitted; quoting U.S. Bill of Rights, First Amendment).
12 *Everson*, 330 U.S. 1, at 13, 15.
13 Ibid., at 14.
14 Ibid., at 15 n. 22.
15 Ibid., at 15.
16 Ibid., at 15–16 (emphasis in original).
17 Ibid., at 16.
18 Ibid., at 18, see also 16.

its relations with groups of religious believers and non-believers; it does not require the state to be their adversary. State power is no more to be used so as to handicap religions than it is to favor them."[19]

Confirmation

Several justices have acknowledged that the Court extended the Establishment Clause to the state level in *Everson*. Black reiterated this recent development in *McCollum v. Board of Education* (1948), flatly stating that "our holding in the *Everson* case [was] that the Fourteenth Amendment made the 'establishment of religion' clause of the First Amendment applicable as a prohibition against the States."[20] Initially, however, a few other justices were not so specific.

Douglas left out *Everson* when citing cases prohibiting "the states from establishing religion or prohibiting its free exercise" in his *Zorach v. Clauson* (1952) opinion.[21] For Justice Tom Clark in *Abington v. Schempp* (1963), *Everson* was among a few other cases that instead regarded *Cantwell* as the decision in which the Court incorporated both First Amendment religious clauses.[22] Justice William Brennan in *Malloy v. Hogan* (1964) and Justice Arthur Goldberg in *Pointer v. Texas* (1965) and *Griswold v. Connecticut* (1965) did not mention *Everson* in their lists of federal rights that the Court held also limited states.[23] Such neglect of *Everson* as the establishment incorporation case, however, was rare and largely dissipated over time. Douglas even made a clearer statement about the case elsewhere.

Some justices have unequivocally confirmed that the Court in *Everson* incorporated the Establishment Clause. In *McGowan v. Maryland* (1961), Chief Justice Earl Warren explained that in *Everson*, the Court "found that the First and Fourteenth Amendments afford protection against religious establishment far more extensive than merely to forbid a national or state church."[24] Returning to Douglas, in his *Lemon v. Kurtzman* (1971) concurrence, he referenced *Everson* as the decision in which the Court extended the right against establishment to the states.[25] In *Wallace v. Jaffree* (1985), Justice John Paul Stevens stated that "[t]he

19 Ibid., at 18.

20 *McCollum v. Board of Education*, 333 U.S. 203, at 211, see also 210 (1948).

21 *Zorach v. Clauson*, 343 U.S. 306, at 309 n. 3 (1952).

22 *School District of Abington Township, Pennsylvania v. Schempp*, 374 U.S. 203, at 215–16 (1963).

23 *Malloy v. Hogan*, 378 U.S. 1, at 5 n. 4 (1964); *Pointer v. Texas*, 380 U.S. 400, at 411–12, 414 (1965) (Goldberg, A., concurring); and *Griswold v. Connecticut*, 381 U.S. 479, at 488 n. 2 (1965) (Goldberg, A., concurring).

24 *McGowan v. Maryland*, 366 U.S. 420, at 442 (1961).

25 *Lemon v. Kurtzman*, 403 U.S. 602, at 640 (1971) (Douglas, W., concurring).

Establishment Clause of the First Amendment, of course, has long been held applicable to the States. *Everson v. Board of Education*."[26] Others who have verified that the Court in *Everson* incorporated the proscription against establishment include Justice Anthony Kennedy in *Lee v. Weisman* (1992), Justice David Souter in his concurring *Lee* opinion, and Justice Samuel Alito in *McDonald v. Chicago* (2010).[27]

Summary

In *Everson*, the Court incorporated the First Amendment right to be free from government establishment of religion. Black in *Everson* asserted that "the Fourteenth Amendment was interpreted to make the prohibitions of the First applicable to state action abridging religious freedom" and "[t]here is every reason to give the same application and broad interpretation to the 'establishment of religion' clause."[28] Several justices addressing this right at the state level since 1947 agree that *Everson* is the establishment incorporation case.

26 *Wallace v. Jaffree*, 472 U.S. 38, at 42 n. 10 (1985).

27 *Lee v. Weisman*, 505 U.S. 577, at 587; 610, 620 (Souter, D., concurring) (1992); and *McDonald v. City of Chicago*, 561 U.S. 742, at 764 n. 12 (2010).

28 *Everson*, 330 U.S. 1, at 15.

Exercise of Religion

"Congress shall make no law [...] prohibiting the free exercise [of religion]."

In *Cantwell v. Connecticut* (1940), the Supreme Court ruled in favor of protecting the First Amendment right to free exercise of religion from state infringement.[1] This decision followed the Court's application to the state level of the First Amendment's guarantees of speech in *Gitlow v. New York* (1925), press in *Near v. Minnesota* (1931), and assembly in *De Jonge v. Oregon* (1937).[2]

Before *Cantwell*

In its early cases addressing free religious exercise, the Court held that the federal right did not extend to the states. It discussed this protection in reference to Congress's extension of First Amendment religious rights to people living in U.S. territories. Did these federal guarantees remain after territories became states? The Court's answer was a resounding "no." As Justice John Catron succinctly

1 *Cantwell v. Connecticut*, 310 U.S. 296 (1940).

2 *Gitlow v. People of New York*, 268 U.S. 652 (1925); *Near v. State of Minnesota ex rel. Olson*, 283 U.S. 697 (1931); and *De Jonge v. Oregon*, 299 U.S. 353 (1937).

stated in *Permoli v. Municipality* (1845), "[t]he Constitution makes no provision for protecting the citizens of the respective states in their religious liberties; this is left to the state constitutions and laws."[3] The Court adhered to this view even after ratification of the Fourteenth Amendment, holding in *Reynolds v. United States* (1879) and *Davis v. Beason* (1890) that the First Amendment prohibited only the federal government, including its territories, from interfering with religious practices.[4]

Around the time of *Gitlow* and *Near*, some justices referred to free exercise of religion as a constitutionally protected "liberty." For Justice James McReynolds in *Meyer v. Nebraska* (1923), the Fourteenth Amendment due process of law protection of "liberty" included the individual rights of occupation, education, marriage, family, and religion.[5] He added that state "police power" could regulate such freedoms, but the interference should not be "arbitrary" or unrelated to the "public interest."[6] In *Hamilton v. Regents of California* (1934), Justice Pierce Butler agreed that the liberty of the Due Process Clause included religious freedom.[7] However, the main purpose of government at any level, he emphasized, is to "preserve itself in adequate strength to maintain peace and order and to assure the just enforcement of law."[8]

In its First Amendment rulings of *Gitlow* for speech, *Near* for press, and *De Jonge* for assembly, the Court appealed to the Due Process Clause protection of liberty to defend federal rights against states. As Justice Edward Sanford in *Gitlow* argued, free speech and press "are among the fundamental personal rights and 'liberties' protected by the due process clause of the Fourteenth Amendment from impairment by the States."[9] The Court used the same approach in *Near*, with Chief Justice Charles Hughes stating "that the liberty of the press, and of speech, is within the liberty safeguarded by the due process clause of the Fourteenth Amendment from invasion by state action."[10] Similarly, he argued in *De Jonge* that peaceful assembly was among the "fundamental principles of liberty and justice" that "the Fourteenth Amendment embodies in the general terms of its due process clause."[11]

3 *Permoli v. Municipality No. 1 of New Orleans*, 44 U.S. (3 How.) 589, at 609 (1845).
4 *Reynolds v. United States*, 98 U.S. 145, at 162, 166 (1879); and *Davis v. Beason*, 133 U.S. 333, at 342, 348 (1890).
5 *Meyer v. Nebraska*, 262 U.S. 390, at 399 (1923).
6 Ibid., at 400.
7 *Hamilton v. Regents of University of California*, 293 U.S. 245, at 262 (1934).
8 Ibid.
9 *Gitlow*, 268 U.S. 652, at 666.
10 *Near*, 283 U.S. 697, at 707.
11 *De Jonge*, 299 U.S. 353, at 364.

The Court affirmed its use of this Due Process reasoning to extend federal rights to the state level in other cases, such as *Schneider v. State* (1939).[12]

Cantwell v. Connecticut (1940)

A unanimous Court held that state governments could not interfere with the First Amendment guarantee of free religious exercise. The issue before the Court was whether a state law requiring government approval for soliciting anything of value from the public for a religion purpose violated the First Amendment rights of speech and religious exercise. The Court focused on religious exercise rather than freedom of speech because the statute regulated the activity of solicitation for a "religious cause."[13]

Authoring the 9-0 opinion, Justice Owen Roberts argued that the Fourteenth Amendment protection of liberty included free religious exercise at the state level. As he explained,

> [w]e hold that the statute, as construed and applied to the appellants, deprives them of their liberty without due process of law in contravention of the Fourteenth Amendment. The fundamental concept of liberty embodied in that Amendment embraces the liberties guaranteed by the First Amendment.[14]

This was the same rationale that the Court used in *Gitlow*, *Near*, and *De Jonge*, with Roberts also suggesting that the Due Process Clause protected the entire First Amendment from state governments. He cited his recent *Schneider* opinion for support.[15]

At one point, Roberts addressed the Bill of Rights' prohibitions on Congress from making laws establishing or interfering with religion and asserted that "[t]he Fourteenth Amendment has rendered the legislatures of the states as incompetent as Congress to enact such laws."[16] However, he focused on religious exercise, elaborating that "[f]reedom of conscience and freedom to adhere to such religious organization or form of worship as the individual may choose cannot be restricted by law."[17] The state law regulating solicitation of funds authorized a government official "to determine whether the cause is a religious one, and that the issue of a

12 *Schneider v. State*, 308 U.S. 147, at 160 n. 8, 161 (1939).
13 *Cantwell*, 310 U.S. 296, at 302.
14 Ibid., at 303.
15 Ibid. (citing *Schneider*, 308 U.S. 147, at 160).
16 *Cantwell*, 310 U.S. 296, at 303.
17 Ibid.

certificate depends upon his affirmative action. If he finds that the cause is not that of religion, to solicit for it becomes a crime."[18] "Such a censorship of religion as the means of determining its right to survive," Roberts reiterated, "is a denial of liberty protected by the First Amendment and included in the liberty which is within the protection of the Fourteenth."[19]

Confirmation

Justices have confirmed that the Court has incorporated the right to free exercise of religion with several crediting *Cantwell* for this development. Occasionally, a justice asserted that the Court in *Cantwell* applied both religious protections to the states, including Justice William Douglas in *Zorach v. Clauson* (1952), Justice Tom Clark in *Abington v. Schempp* (1963), and Justice Sandra Day O'Connor in her concurring *Wallace v. Jaffree* (1985) opinion.[20] Justice Hugo Black in *Gideon v. Wainwright* (1963) and Justice William Brennan in *Malloy v. Hogan* (1964) each cited the case for incorporation of "religion," rather than a specific clause.[21] A few justices simply identified *Cantwell* along with other incorporation cases without distinguishing which rights each one protected, such as Justice Potter Stewart in *Edwards v. South Carolina* (1963) and Justice Arthur Goldberg in his *Pointer v. Texas* (1965) and *Griswold v. Connecticut* (1965) concurrences.[22] In *Everson v. Board of Education* (1947), Black listed *Cantwell* and other cases in which the Court used the Fourteenth Amendment to protect religious practice against states.[23]

A few justices, however, have recognized that the Court applied the right of religious freedom to the state level in *Cantwell*. Brennan in *Sherbert v. Verner* (1963) mentioned that "[t]he door of the Free Exercise Clause stands tightly closed against any governmental regulation of religious *beliefs* as such, *Cantwell*

18 Ibid., at 305.

19 Ibid.

20 *Zorach v. Clauson*, 343 U.S. 306, at 309 n. 3 (1952); *School District of Abington Township, Pennsylvania v. Schempp*, 374 U.S. 203, at 215 (1963); and *Wallace v. Jaffree*, 472 U.S. 38, at 67–68 (1985) (O'Connor, S., concurring).

21 *Gideon v. Wainwright*, 372 U.S. 335, at 341 n. 4 (1963); and *Malloy v. Hogan*, 378 U.S. 1, at 5 n. 4 (1964).

22 *Edwards v. South Carolina*, 372 U.S. 229, at 235 (1963); *Pointer v. Texas*, 380 U.S. 400, at 411–12, 414 (1965) (Goldberg, A., concurring); and *Griswold v. Connecticut*, 381 U.S. 479, at 488 n. 2 (1965) (Goldberg, A., concurring).

23 *Everson v. Board of Education of the Township of Ewing*, 330 U.S. 1, at 15 n. 22 (1947).

v. Connecticut."[24] Other confirmations of *Cantwell* as the free religion incorporation case include Justice John Paul Stevens in *Wallace*, Justice Anthony Kennedy in *Church of the Lukumi Babalu Aye v. Hialeah* (1993), Justice David Souter in his concurrence of that case, and Justice Samuel Alito in his listing of incorporated rights in *McDonald v. Chicago* (2010).[25]

Summary

The Court in *Cantwell* protected the First Amendment right to free exercise of religion from state interference. Roberts held that "[f]reedom of conscience and freedom to adhere to such religious organization or form of worship as the individual may choose cannot be restricted by law."[26] Some justices have since acknowledged that the Court in *Cantwell* extended religious exercise to the states.

24 *Sherbert v. Verner*, 374 U.S. 398, at 402 (1963) (emphasis in original).

25 *Wallace*, 472 U.S. 38, at 49 n. 34 (1985); *Church of the Lukumi Babalu Aye, Inc. v. City of Hialeah*, 508 U.S. 520, at 531; 569 (Souter, D., concurring) (1993); and *McDonald v. City of Chicago*, 561 U.S. 742, at 761, see also 764 n. 12 (2010).

26 *Cantwell*, 310 U.S. 296, at 303.

Freedom of Speech

"Congress shall make no law [...] abridging the freedom of speech."

The Supreme Court in *Gitlow v. New York* (1925) asserted that the Due Process Clause of the Fourteenth Amendment could protect freedom of speech from state suppression.[1] While this case also addressed other First Amendment guarantees as applicable to the state level, the Court focused on speech. In its defense of what it also referred to as free expression, the *Gitlow* majority reversed an earlier ruling that the federal right of free speech did not restrain state governments.

Before *Gitlow*

Just a few years before *Gitlow*, the Court expressly ruled against extending the right of free speech to the states in *Prudential Insurance v. Cheek* (1922). Justice Mahlon Pitney argued that the petitioner failed to demonstrate the relevancy of the Due Process Clause, and that the Privileges or Immunities Clause only prevented states from violating federal rights, not those "inherent in state citizenship," as the Court

1 *Gitlow v. People of New York*, 268 U.S. 652 (1925).

ruled in *Slaughter-House Cases* (1873) and other decisions.[2] The federal guarantee of free speech did not pertain to states. As Pitney unequivocally stated, "neither the Fourteenth Amendment nor any other provision of the Constitution of the United States imposes upon the States any restrictions about 'freedom of speech' or the 'liberty of silence.'"[3]

Elsewhere, however, the Court formulated a due process rationale for defending federal rights at the state level. Justice William Moody in *Twining v. New Jersey* (1908) asserted that the Due Process Clause of the Fourteenth Amendment could protect "fundamental rights" against state government. He argued that "it is possible that some of the personal rights safeguarded by the first eight Amendments against National action may also be safeguarded against state action, because a denial of them would be a denial of due process of law," citing *Chicago, Burlington & Quincy Railroad v. Chicago* (1897) for support.[4] In *Meyer v. Nebraska* (1923), Justice James McReynolds added that constitutional protection of "fundamental rights" included people who did not speak English.[5]

Gitlow v. New York (1925)

In its 7-2 *Gitlow* decision, the Court argued that due process of law, which the Fourteenth Amendment guaranteed at the state level, involved the fundamental right of free speech. The background of this case involved a state law that prohibited criminal anarchy, which the state defined in part as advocating, through speaking or writing, the illegal or violent overthrow of government. The state accused the defendant of advocating, advising, and teaching the unlawful overthrow of government for publishing and distributing a written piece promoting revolution; he also spoke at a few Socialist Party branches in the state.[6] The Court pointed out that the indictments were about "advocacy" rather than "abstract 'doctrine' or academic discussion."[7]

2 *Prudential Insurance Co. v. Cheek*, 259 U.S. 530, at 539 (1922) (citing *Slaughter-House Cases*, 83 U.S. (16 Wall.) 36 (1873)).
3 *Prudential*, 259 U.S. 530, at 543.
4 *Twining v. State of New Jersey*, 211 U.S. 78, at 99 (1908) (citing *Chicago, Burlington & Quincy Railroad Co. v. Chicago*, 166 U.S. 226 (1897)).
5 *Meyer v. Nebraska*, 262 U.S. 390, at 401 (1923).
6 *Gitlow*, 268 U.S. 652, at 654–59.
7 Ibid., at 664–65.

The incorporation of free speech is bound up with the Court's argument that the Due Process Clause protection of liberty included fundamental rights. As Justice Edward Sanford explained in the *Gitlow* opinion,

> [f]or present purposes we may and do assume that freedom of speech and of the press—which are protected by the First Amendment from abridgment by Congress—are among the fundamental personal rights and "liberties" protected by the due process clause of the Fourteenth Amendment from impairment by the States.[8]

Importantly, he dismissed the 1922 *Prudential* view that the right of free speech did not apply at the state level as an "incidental statement."[9] After all, freedom of speech was a fundamental right. As such, Sanford explained in reference to several cases including *Twining* and *Meyer*, due process of law demanded its protection against state suppression.[10] For Sanford, "the 'liberty' protected by the Fourteenth Amendment includes the liberty of speech and of the press," which he also referred to as the "liberty of expression."[11] He elaborated that, while subject to government restrictions for the sake of preserving public order, "this freedom is an inestimable privilege in a free government."[12]

The Court assumed that the Fourteenth Amendment protected the fundamental rights of speech and press from state invasion. In rejecting *Prudential*, its focus was on speech. However, this application of speech at the state level was the Court's perspective, not its ruling. *Gitlow* provided a much stronger defense of government's use of "police powers" to maintain peace and safety than it did of free expression.[13] In the end, the Court upheld the state law prohibiting criminal anarchy.

Confirmation

While the Court has recognized the Due Process Clause as encompassing free speech, only a few justices have clearly credited *Gitlow* as the incorporation case. This is not surprising since Sanford in *Gitlow* assumed rather than held that the Due Process Clause protected speech and press against states, referred to these two rights as "free expression," and ruled in favor of the New York criminal anarchy law.

8 Ibid., at 666.
9 Ibid.
10 Ibid., at 666 n. 9 (citing *Twining*, 211 U.S. 78, at 108; and *Meyer*, 262 U.S. 390, at 399).
11 *Gitlow*, 268 U.S. 652, at 664.
12 Ibid., at 667.
13 Ibid.

Moreover, just two years later, the Court focused on the right of speech in *Whitney v. California* (1927).

Authoring the *Whitney* opinion, Sanford presented the First Amendment right of free speech as immune from state violation, but his emphasis was again on government authority to prevent speech from going too far. Using nearly the same passages from *Gitlow* but without mentioning press, he explained that the Court in that decision held "[t]hat the freedom of speech which is secured by the Constitution does not confer an absolute right to speak [...] and that a State in the exercise of its police power may punish those who abuse this freedom."[14] In *Fiske v. Kansas* (1927), Sanford implied the same, mentioning *Gitlow* in relation to a state law prohibiting seditious speech.[15] While he referenced *Gitlow* in these opinions, Sanford did not state that it was the case in which the Court protected speech against state abridgment.

Some justices have listed several cases along with *Gitlow* as those in which the Court extended freedom of speech to the states. These diluted references are usually made in discussions about the Court's due process defense of federal rights at the state level. For example, Justice Louis Brandeis in his *Whitney* concurrence cited several cases including *Gitlow* in which the Court had incorporated speech because "fundamental rights comprised within the term liberty are protected by the federal Constitution from invasion by the states."[16] Chief Justice Charles Hughes in *Stromberg v. California* (1931) stated that "[i]t has been determined that the conception of liberty under the due process clause of the Fourteenth Amendment embraces the right of free speech" and he listed *Gitlow* as the first case in which the Court incorporated the right, followed by *Whitney* and *Fiske*.[17] Some other justices who credit more than one case along with *Gitlow* for incorporation of free speech include Justice Stanley Reed in *Jones v. Opelika* (1943), Justice John Harlan II in *NAACP v. Alabama* (1958) and *Shelton v. Tucker* (1960), Justice Potter Stewart in *Edwards v. South Carolina* (1963), and Justice Arthur Goldberg in *Pointer v. Texas* (1965) and *Griswold v. Connecticut* (1965).[18] Others have presented speech and press together and asserted that the Court in several cases including *Gitlow*

14 *Whitney v. California*, 274 U.S. 357, at 371 (1927).

15 *Fiske v. Kansas*, 274 U.S. 380, at 386 (1927).

16 *Whitney*, at 373 (Brandeis, L., concurring).

17 *Stromberg v. California*, 283 U.S. 359, at 368 (1931).

18 *Jones v. Opelika*, 319 U.S. 103, at 120–21, 126 n. 11 (1943) (Reed, S., dissenting); *NAACP v. Alabama ex rel. Patterson*, 357 U.S. 449, at 460 (1958); *Shelton v. Tucker*, 364 U.S. 479, at 497 (1960) (Harlan, J., dissenting); *Edwards v. South Carolina*, 372 U.S. 229, at 235 (1963); *Pointer v. Texas*, 380 U.S. 400, at 412 n. 2 (1965) (Goldberg, A., concurring); and *Griswold v. Connecticut*, 381 U.S. 479, at 488 n. 2 (1965) (Goldberg, A., concurring).

protected these rights against state governments.[19] For Justice Hugo Black in *Gideon v. Wainwright* (1963) and Justice William Brennan in *Malloy v. Hogan* (1964), the Court in *Gitlow* incorporated both speech and press.[20]

However, a few justices have clearly stated that the Court in *Gitlow* incorporated the right of free speech. In his *Terminiello v. Chicago* (1949) dissent, Justice Robert Jackson stated in relation to the constitutional protection of free speech that "state power is bound by the same limitation as Congress. *Gitlow v. New York*."[21] Goldberg in his *New York Times v. Sullivan* (1964) concurrence explained that "[i]t was not until *Gitlow v. New York*, decided in 1925, that it was intimated that the freedom of speech guaranteed by the First Amendment was applicable to the States by reason of the Fourteenth Amendment."[22] Justice Samuel Alito in *McDonald v. Chicago* (2010) recognized *Gitlow* as the free speech incorporation case.[23]

Summary

For the *Gitlow* majority, the Due Process Clause protection of liberty from state interference included the First Amendment right of free speech. Sanford agreed with the defendant's proposition "[t]hat the 'liberty' protected by the Fourteenth Amendment includes the liberty of speech and of the press."[24] The Court ruled against its *Prudential* holding that the Fourteenth Amendment did not protect the federal right of free speech against states. A few justices addressing this guarantee since 1925 confirm that *Gitlow* is the case in which the Court incorporated freedom of speech.

19 See, for example, *Near v. State of Minnesota ex rel. Olson*, 283 U.S. 697, at 707; 723–24 (Butler, P. dissenting) (1931); *Grosjean v. American Press Co., Inc.*, 297 U.S. 233, at 244 (1936); *De Jonge v. Oregon*, 299 U.S. 353, at 364 (1937); *Lovell v. City of Griffin*, 303 U.S. 444, at 450 (1938); and *Schneider v. State*, 308 U.S. 147, at 160 n. 8 (1939).

20 *Gideon v. Wainwright*, 372 U.S. 335, at 341 n. 4 (1963); and *Malloy v. Hogan*, 378 U.S. 1, at 5 n. 4 (1964).

21 *Terminiello v. Chicago*, 337 U.S. 1, at 29 (1949).

22 *New York Times Co. v. Sullivan*, 376 U.S. 254, at 299 n. 3 (1964) (Goldberg, A., concurring; citation information omitted).

23 *McDonald v. City of Chicago*, 561 U.S. 742, at 764 n. 12 (2010).

24 *Gitlow*, 268 U.S. 652, at 664.

Freedom of the Press

"Congress shall make no law [...] abridging the freedom [...] of the press."

The Supreme Court incorporated freedom of the press in *Near v. Minnesota* (1931).[1] Out of all its guarantees, the Bill of Rights only describes press, as well as speech, as a "freedom," although justices have sometimes referred to all First Amendment protections as freedoms. In defending the free press right at the state level, the Court adhered to the same Due Process Clause rationale that Justice Edward Sanford used to protect speech against state interference in *Gitlow v. New York* (1925).[2]

Before *Near*

In early cases regarding freedom of the press, the Court held that the right protected against the federal government imposing "prior restraint," unless a publication endangered public order and safety. As Justice Oliver Wendell Holmes in *Patterson v. Colorado* (1907) explained, "even if we were to assume that freedom of speech

1 *Near v. State of Minnesota ex rel. Olson*, 283 U.S. 697 (1931).
2 *Gitlow v. People of New York*, 268 U.S. 652 (1925).

and freedom of the press were protected from abridgments on the part not only of the United States, but also of the states," the First Amendment protection of press would only prevent "previous restraints upon publications," except on those "deemed contrary to the public welfare."[3] In the free press case of *Schenck v. United States* (1919), Holmes elaborated that "[i]t well may be that the prohibition of laws abridging the freedom of speech is not confined to previous restraints, although to prevent them may have been the main purpose."[4] He famously held that government may suppress public expressions if "the words used are used in such circumstances and are of such a nature as to create a clear and present danger that they will bring about the substantive evils that Congress has a right to prevent."[5]

Before *Near*, however, the Court developed a Fourteenth Amendment Due Process Clause defense of civil liberties. In *Twining v. New Jersey* (1908), Justice William Moody argued that some Bill of Rights' protections were essential to due process of law and therefore might be immune from state invasion.[6] In *Gitlow*, Sanford elaborated that the Fourteenth Amendment mandate that no state may deprive individual "liberty" without following due process of law encompassed "fundamental personal rights and 'liberties,'" among which he included speech and press.[7] The Court affirmed that the Due Process Clause protection of liberty encompassed fundamental rights, including in *Whitney v. California* (1927), *Fiske v. Kansas* (1927), and *Stromberg v. California* (1931).[8] When the Court heard *Near*, it had a theoretical defense available for applying substantive federal rights to the state level.

Near v. Minnesota (1931)

In *Near*, the Court incorporated the First Amendment right to freedom of the press. This case concerned a state law that in part authorized prosecution of anyone publishing and circulating any "malicious, scandalous and defamatory newspaper, magazine or other periodical."[9] It also permitted government officials to

3 *Patterson v. Colorado*, 205 U.S. 454, at 462 (1907).
4 *Schenck v. United States*, 249 U.S. 47, at 51–52 (1919).
5 Ibid., at 52.
6 *Twining v. State of New Jersey*, 211 U.S. 78, at 99, 106–7 (1908).
7 *Gitlow*, 268 U.S. 652, at 666.
8 *Whitney v. California*, 274 U.S. 357, at 373 (1927) (Brandeis, L., concurring); *Fiske v. Kansas*, 274 U.S. 380, at 386–87 (1927); and *Stromberg v. California*, 283 U.S. 359, at 368, 369 (1931).
9 *Near*, 283 U.S. 697, at 702.

prevent any person found guilty of such a "nuisance" from further publication and distribution.

The Court held that the Due Process Clause protected the fundamental right of free press at the state level. In the 5-4 *Near* opinion, Chief Justice Charles Hughes stated that

> [i]t is no longer open to doubt that the liberty of the press, and of speech, is within the liberty safeguarded by the due process clause of the Fourteenth Amendment from invasion by state action. It was found impossible to conclude that this essential personal liberty of the citizen was left unprotected by the general guaranty of fundamental rights of person and property.[10]

This was to say that the Due Process Clause protection of "life, liberty, or property" encompassed "fundamental rights," including press and speech. Hughes referenced the free speech cases of *Gitlow*, *Whitney*, *Fiske*, and *Stromberg* as examples in which the Court appealed to the same due process defense of fundamental rights.[11] It now used it to protect freedom of the press at the state level.

For the Court, the right of free press prevented prior restraint on publication, thereby protecting individuals against government suppression of liberty.[12] Hughes argued "that liberty of the press, historically considered and taken up by the Federal Constitution, has meant, principally although not exclusively, immunity from previous restraints or censorship."[13] He ruled that the state law forbidding publications that defamed public officials, true or not, was "an infringement of the liberty of the press guaranteed by the Fourteenth Amendment."[14]

Confirmation

The Court has recognized that the Fourteenth Amendment protects the right of free press against state violation but did not at first clearly refer to *Near* as the incorporation case. Some of these ambiguous confirmations were part of broader discussions about incorporation theory. In *Grosjean v. American Press* (1936), for example, Justice George Sutherland explained

10 Ibid., at 707.

11 Ibid. (citing *Gitlow*, 268 U.S. 652, at 666; *Whitney*, 274 U.S. 357, at 362; *Fiske*, 274 U.S. 380, at 382; and *Stromberg*, 283 U.S. 359).

12 *Near*, 283 U.S. 697, at 712.

13 Ibid., at 716.

14 Ibid., at 723.

> [t]hat freedom of speech and of the press are rights of the same fundamental character, safeguarded by the due process of law clause of the Fourteenth Amendment against abridgement by state legislation, has likewise been settled by a series of decisions of this Court beginning with *Gitlow v. New York* and ending with *Near v. Minnesota*.[15]

In *Lovell v. Griffin* (1938), Hughes referenced *Gitlow*, *Stromberg*, *Near*, *Grosjean*, and *De Jonge v. Oregon* (1937) as cases in which the Court used the Fourteenth Amendment to protect the "the fundamental personal rights and liberties" of speech and press.[16] These justices included other cases for support of the due process defense of fundamental rights and did not directly state that the Court in *Near* incorporated free press.

Some justices identifying incorporation cases have ignored *Near* in reference to free press. Justice Hugo Black in *Gideon v. Wainwright* (1963) referenced *Grosjean* as the incorporation case for press.[17] Justice William Brennan in a *Malloy v. Hogan* (1964) footnote credited the Court for incorporating "speech and press" in *Gitlow*, *Lovell*, and *New York Times v. Sullivan* (1964) and "press" in *Grosjean*.[18] The Court, however, did not extend free press to the state level in any of these cases.

The sparsity of references to *Near* as the free press incorporation case may be due to its focus on prior restraint. Justices have often described the right to freedom of the press as a prohibition against prior restraint. Chief Justice Warren Burger stated in *Organization for a Better Austin v. Keefe* (1971) that "[u]nder *Near v. Minnesota* (1931), the injunction, so far as it imposes prior restraint on speech and publication, constitutes an impermissible restraint on First Amendment rights."[19] Government must demonstrate a "heavy burden" to silence an expected publication, such as trying to prevent interference with traffic, physical altercations, and other disturbances of the peace.[20] This is to say, as some justices have, that protection from prior restraint is not absolute.[21] In *Nebraska Press Association v. Stuart* (1976), Burger explained that, following *Near* and other press cases, the Court

15 *Grosjean v. American Press Co., Inc.*, 297 U.S. 233, at 244 (1936) (citation information omitted).

16 *Lovell v. City of Griffin*, 303 U.S. 444, at 450 (1938) (citing *Gitlow*, 268 U.S. 652, at 666; *Stromberg*, 283 U.S. 359, at 368; *Near*, 283 U.S. 697, at 707; *Grosjean*, 297 U.S. 233, at 244; and *De Jonge v. Oregon*, 299 U.S. 353, at 364 (1937)).

17 *Gideon v. Wainwright*, 372 U.S. 335, at 341–42 (1963).

18 *Malloy v. Hogan*, 378 U.S. 1, at 5 n. 4 (1964) (citing *Gitlow*, 268 U.S. 652, 666; *Lovell*, 303 U.S. 444, 450; *New York Times Co. v. Sullivan*, 376 U.S. 254 (1964); and *Grosjean*, 297 U.S. 233, 244).

19 *Organization for a Better Austin v. Keefe*, 402 U.S. 415, at 418 (1971) (citation information omitted).

20 Ibid., 417–19.

21 See *Kingsley Books, Inc. v. Brown*, 354 U.S. 436, at 441 (1957); and *Nebraska Press Association v. Stuart*, 427 U.S. 539, at 570 (1976).

interpreted freedom of the press to mean "special protection against orders that prohibit the publication or broadcast of particular information or commentary—orders that impose a 'previous' or 'prior' restraint on speech."[22] These and other references could be taken as confirmations that the Court in *Near* incorporated freedom of the press; however, freedom from prior restraint is narrower than the right of free press.

Justices have provided a few acknowledgments that the Court in *Near* extended free press to the state level. Returning to Burger in *Nebraska Press*, while he explained that the Court regarded the First Amendment right as preventing unjust prior restraint, he also wrote that

> [t]he First Amendment provides that "Congress shall make no law ... abridging the freedom ... of the press," and it is "no longer open to doubt that the liberty of the press, and of speech, is within the liberty safeguarded by the due process clause of the Fourteenth Amendment from invasion by state action." *Near v. Minnesota*.[23]

Justice John Paul Stevens in *Wallace v. Jaffree* (1985) stated that the Court in *Near* protected the "right to publish an unpopular newspaper" against state interference.[24] In *McDonald v. Chicago* (2010), Justice Samuel Alito included "*Near v. Minnesota ex rel. Olson* (1931) (freedom of the press)" in his list of incorporated rights.[25]

Summary

The Court in *Near* incorporated freedom of the press with the same rationale that it had used in *Gitlow* to protect speech. As Hughes ruled in *Near*, "the liberty of the press [is] guaranteed by the Fourteenth Amendment."[26] The Court has affirmed that it applied the First Amendment right of free press to the states, with some confirmations providing more clarity than others.

22 *Nebraska Press*, 427 U.S. 539, at 556.
23 Ibid. (ellipses in original; quoting *Near*, 283 U.S. 697, at 707).
24 *Wallace v. Jaffree*, 472 U.S. 38, at 49 n. 34 (1985).
25 *McDonald v. City of Chicago*, 561 U.S. 742, at 764 n. 12 (2010).
26 *Near*, 283 U.S. 697, at 723.

Peaceably Assemble

> "Congress shall make no law [...] abridging [...] the right of the people peaceably to assemble."

In *De Jonge v. Oregon* (1937), the Supreme Court incorporated the right of the people to peacefully assemble.[1] Along with a few other guarantees, the Bill of Rights describes assembly as a "right of the people." The Court in *De Jonge* appealed to the First Amendment rights of speech and press along with the due process protection of fundamental rights rationale to apply the assembly guarantee to the state level.

Before *De Jonge*

At first, the Court dismissed and restricted the peaceful assembly right at the state level. When addressing it in *United States v. Cruikshank* (1876), the Court followed its *Barron v. Baltimore* (1833) interpretation of the Bill of Rights as pressing only upon the federal government.[2] Later decisions mentioned the right

1 *De Jonge v. Oregon*, 299 U.S. 353 (1937).

2 *United States v. Cruikshank*, 92 U.S. 542, at 552 (1876) (citing *Barron ex rel. Tiernan v. City of Baltimore*, 32 U.S. (7 Pet.) 243, at 250 (1833)).

to assemble along with speech, holding that governments could restrict both for the sake of preserving public safety. For example, Justice Edward Sanford argued in *Whitney v. California* (1927) that a state's restriction on speech and assembly by individuals who were "menacing the peace and welfare of the State" was not "unwarrantably infringing any right of free speech, assembly or association."[3] Justice Louis Brandeis in his concurring *Whitney* opinion agreed that these rights were not "absolute" and "[t]heir exercise is subject to restriction"; however, he defended free speech and assembly as "fundamental rights" that the Due Process Clause protected from a state's "denial of liberty."[4]

While the Court in *Gitlow v. New York* (1925) and *Near v. Minnesota* (1931) respectively protected speech and press against state governments, it had not incorporated other First Amendment rights. In these rulings, however, the Court argued that the due process defense of liberty included fundamental rights.[5] It recognized this due process rationale in other cases, including *Stromberg v. California* (1931), *Hamilton v. Regents of California* (1934) and *Grosjean v. American Press* (1936).[6]

De Jonge v. Oregon (1937)

The Court unanimously ruled in *De Jonge* that the right to peaceably assemble applied at the state level. The case addressed the state using its criminal syndicalism law—part of which prohibited gatherings promoting unlawful means to change government—to charge some people who attended a Communist Party meeting.

Chief Justice Charles Hughes appealed to the due process protection of fundamental rights to extend peaceful assembly to the state level. He contended that

> [f]reedom of speech and of the press are fundamental rights which are safeguarded by the due process clause of the Fourteenth Amendment of the Federal Constitution. The right of peaceable assembly is a right cognate to those of free speech and free press and is equally fundamental.[7]

3 *Whitney v. California*, 274 U.S. 357, at 372 (1927).
4 Ibid., at 373, 374 (Brandeis, L., concurring).
5 *Gitlow v. People of New York*, 268 U.S. 652, at 666 (1925); and *Near v. State of Minnesota ex rel. Olson*, 283 U.S. 697, at 707 (1931).
6 *Stromberg v. California*, 283 U.S. 359, at 368 (1931); *Hamilton v. Regents of University of California*, 293 U.S. 245, at 262 (1934); and *Grosjean v. American Press Co., Inc.*, 297 U.S. 233, at 243, 244 (1936).
7 *De Jonge*, 299 U.S. 353, at 364 (citation information omitted).

Hughes referenced *Gitlow*, *Stromberg*, *Near*, and *Grosjean* for support of the Due Process Clause defense of fundamental rights.[8] Assembly, speech, and press were interrelated because they were each fundamental.

Regarding peaceful assembly, Hughes argued that "[t]he First Amendment of the Federal Constitution expressly guarantees that right against abridgment by Congress. But explicit mention there does not argue exclusion elsewhere."[9] The right to assemble, he argued, "cannot be denied without violating those fundamental principles of liberty and justice which lie at the base of all civil and political institutions,—principles which the Fourteenth Amendment embodies in the general terms of its due process clause."[10] Hughes held that "consistently with the Federal Constitution, peaceable assembly for lawful discussion cannot be made a crime."[11]

Like other rights, people may use peaceful assembly to help them control government. The purpose of speech, press, and assembly rights, Hughes explained, is "to maintain the opportunity for free political discussion, to the end that government may be responsive to the will of the people and that changes, if desired, may be obtained by peaceful means."[12] As all governments throughout the United States were constitutional republics, these rights existed at both federal and state levels. A state may not charge someone for "mere participation in a peaceable assembly and a lawful public discussion," Hughes reiterated.[13]

Confirmation

Since *De Jonge*, the Court has stated that it incorporated the right of peaceful assembly although at first only obliquely crediting the 1937 decision. In *Hague v. CIO* (1939), for example, Justice Owen Roberts stated in reference to a meeting about organizing labor unions that "it is clear that the right peaceably to assemble and to discuss these topics, and to communicate respecting them, whether orally or in writing, is a privilege inherent in citizenship of the United States which the [Fourteenth] Amendment protects."[14] Yet, he did not cite any recent decisions in

8 Ibid. (citing *Gitlow*, 268 U.S. 652, at 666; *Stromberg*, 283 U.S. 359, at 368; *Near*, 283 U.S. 697, at 707; and *Grosjean*, 297 U.S. 233, at 243)).

9 *De Jonge*, 299 U.S. 353, at 364.

10 Ibid.

11 Ibid., at 365.

12 Ibid.

13 Ibid.

14 *Hague v. Committee for Industrial Organization*, 307 U.S. 496, at 513 (1939)

which the Court extended these rights to the state level. Justice Harlan Stone in his *Hague* concurrence more accurately described that the Court had often affirmed, "without a dissenting voice, that freedom of speech and of assembly for any lawful purpose are rights of personal liberty secured to all persons, without regard to citizenship, by the due process clause of the Fourteenth Amendment."[15] Rather than recognizing any single case for incorporating speech or assembly, however, Stone referenced several speech, press, and assembly cases, among which was *De Jonge*.

Some justices referred to several First Amendment protections as an amalgamated group of rights, reflecting the *De Jonge* view that assembly was connected to speech and press. For example, in *Thomas v. Collins* (1945), Justice Wiley Rutledge argued that First Amendment rights were listed together because "[a]ll these, though not identical, are inseparable. They are cognate rights, cf. *De Jonge v. Oregon*, and therefore are united in the First Article's assurance."[16] Similarly, Justice John Harlan II in *NAACP v. Alabama* (1958) explained that the Court commented "upon the close nexus between the freedoms of speech and assembly. *De Jonge v. Oregon*."[17] These kinds of statements are hazy as to whether *De Jonge* incorporated more than one right or asserted First Amendment protections as entangled. Justice Hugo Black elaborated in *Gideon v. Wainwright* (1963) that the Court had incorporated all First Amendment rights and identified *De Jonge* for "assembly," although he also listed *Edwards v. South Carolina* (1963) for "speech, assembly, petition for redress of grievances."[18] At a minimum the Court in these references regarded assembly, like several other First Amendment rights, as immune from state suppression.

A few justices have stated that the Court extended "association" to the states. For Harlan in *NAACP*, "[e]ffective advocacy of both public and private points of view, particularly controversial ones, is undeniably enhanced by group association," for which he credited *De Jonge* followed by *Thomas*.[19] Justice Potter Stewart in *Shelton v. Tucker* (1960), a case about a state requirement that teachers reveal any organizational connections, cited *De Jonge* for protecting "free association."[20] Whether "association" means "assembly" for the Court is debatable. In these instances, however, justices referred to association in terms of organizations.

15 Ibid., at 519 (Stone, H., concurring).

16 *Thomas v. Collins*, 323 U.S. 516, at 530, see also 539 (1945) (citation information omitted).

17 *NAACP v. Alabama ex rel. Patterson*, 357 U.S. 449, at 460 (1958).

18 *Gideon v. Wainwright*, 372 U.S. 335, at 341 n. 4 (1963) (citation information omitted; citing *De Jonge*, 299 U.S. 353, at 394; and *Edwards v. South Carolina*, 372 U.S. 229 (1963)).

19 Ibid. (citing *De Jonge*, 299 U.S. 353, at 364; and *Thomas*, 323 U.S. 516, at 530).

20 *Shelton v. Tucker*, 364 U.S. 479, at 486; see also 497 (Harlan, J., dissenting) (1960).

However, more than one justice has confirmed *De Jonge* as the case in which the Court extended the peaceful assembly guarantee to the state level. Black in his *Adamson v. California* (1947) dissent listed "freedom of assembly, *De Jonge v. Oregon*," among the "fundamental rights" that the Court had used the Fourteenth Amendment to protect from states.[21] In his inventory of incorporated rights in *Malloy v. Hogan* (1964), Justice William Brennan recognized *De Jonge* for "assembly."[22] Justice Samuel Alito in *McDonald v. Chicago* (2010) included in his detailed list of incorporated rights, "*De Jonge v. Oregon* (1937) (freedom of assembly)."[23]

Summary

In *De Jonge*, the Court incorporated the First Amendment right of the people to peacefully assemble. It held that the Due Process Clause protected the right against state incursion. Hughes argued that "[t]he right of peaceable assembly is a right cognate to those of free speech and free press and is equally fundamental."[24] Consequently, he ruled that "peaceable assembly for lawful discussion cannot be made a crime."[25] Following this decision, several justices agreed that the right existed at the state level with a few identifying *De Jonge* as the incorporation case.

21 *Adamson v. California*, 332 U.S. 46, at 84 (1947) (Black, H., dissenting).
22 *Malloy v. Hogan*, 378 U.S. 1, at 5 n. 4 (1964).
23 *McDonald v. City of Chicago*, 561 U.S. 742, at 764 n. 12, see also 761 (2010) (citation information omitted).
24 *De Jonge*, 299 U.S. 353, at 364.
25 Ibid., at 365.

Petition Government

> "Congress shall make no law [...] abridging [...] the right of the people [...] to petition the Government for a redress of grievances."

The right "to petition the government for a redress of grievances" overlaps with the other First Amendment "right of the people," assembly. While the Supreme Court occasionally mentioned petitioning before *Edwards v. South Carolina* (1963), it did not extend the federal right to the state level until then.[1]

Before *Edwards*

When initially addressing the First Amendment guarantee of petitioning, the Court held that it protected people against the federal government; however, it also regarded this right as intrinsic to all republican governments. Among national "privileges and immunities" of citizens, Justice Samuel Miller in *Slaughter-House Cases* (1873) listed "[t]he right to peaceably assemble and petition for redress of grievances."[2] States had their own privileges and immunities, "which belong to

1 *Edwards v. South Carolina*, 372 U.S. 229 (1963).
2 *Slaughter-House Cases*, 83 U.S. (16 Wall.) 36, at 79 (1873).

citizens of the States as such, and that they are left to the State governments for security and protection," not to the Fourteenth Amendment.[3] In *United States v. Cruikshank* (1876), Justice Morrison Waite explained that, while First Amendment rights were national, "[t]he very idea of a government, republican in form, implies a right on the part of its citizens to meet peaceably for consultation in respect to public affairs and to petition for a redress of grievances."[4] He presented one of the earlier theoretical defenses of rights at the state level, arguing that the due process protection of the Fourteenth Amendment "furnishes an additional guaranty against any encroachment by the States upon the fundamental rights which belong to every citizen as a member of society."[5] Nevertheless, Waite stated that the right of petitioning "was not intended to limit the powers of the State governments in respect to their own citizens, but to operate upon the National government alone," for which he cited several cases, leading with *Barron v. Baltimore* (1833).[6]

Justice Owen Roberts in *Hague v. CIO* (1939) defended the First Amendment rights of speech and assembly as protected by the Privileges or Immunities Clause of the Fourteenth Amendment, quoting *Slaughter-House* and *Cruikshank* for support.[7] While the Court in those passages mentioned petitioning along with assembly, it was defending those rights at the federal level. In his concurrence, Justice Harlan Stone confirmed that the Court in *Hague* was addressing assembly and speech and clarified that "the right of citizens to assemble for the purpose of petitioning Congress for the redress of grievances is a privilege of United States citizenship protected by the privileges and immunities clause," for which he too cited *Cruikshank*.[8]

The Court mentioned petitioning government in a few cases that addressed federal rights at the state level. Chief Justice Charles Hughes in *De Jonge v. Oregon* (1937) embraced the Due Process Clause protection of fundamental rights to defend peaceful assembly against states and—in agreement with Waite's view in *Cruikshank*—that people in America may assemble to petition government for a redress of grievances.[9] Justice Wiley Rutledge in *Thomas v. Collins* (1945) agreed that petition stood alongside incorporated rights. Referencing *De Jonge*, he argued

3 Ibid., at 78.
4 *United States v. Cruikshank*, 92 U.S. 542, at 552 (1876).
5 Ibid., at 554.
6 Ibid., at 552 (citing *Barron ex rel. Tiernan v. City of Baltimore*, 32 U.S. (7 Pet.) 243, at 250 (1833)).
7 *Hague v. Committee for Industrial Organization*, 307 U.S. 496, at 512–13 (1939) (citing *Slaughter-House*, 83 U.S. 36; and *Cruikshank*, 92 U.S. 542).
8 *Hague*, 307 U.S. 496, at 522 (Stone, H., concurring; citing *Cruikshank*, 92 U.S. 552–53).
9 *De Jonge v. Oregon*, 299 U.S. 353, at 364 (1937) (citing *Cruikshank*, 92 U.S. 542, at 552).

that speech, press, assembly, and petition "though not identical, are inseparable. They are cognate rights."[10] Yet, the Court did not apply petitioning to the state level in either *De Jonge* or *Thomas*.

The Court pushed these defenses of petitioning forward as it heard cases about the rights of group members. Justice John Harlan II in *NAACP v. Alabama* (1958), a case about association, agreed that the Due Process Clause protected several First Amendment rights from state governments. Referencing both *De Jonge* and *Thomas*, he argued that "[e]ffective advocacy of both public and private points of view, particularly controversial ones, is undeniably enhanced by group association" and, citing *Gitlow v. New York* (1925) followed by other cases, "that freedom to engage in association for the advancement of beliefs and ideas is an inseparable aspect of the 'liberty' assured by the Due Process Clause of the Fourteenth Amendment."[11] While Harlan did not mention petition, his use of "advocacy" and "advancement of beliefs and ideas" by a group calling on government to change discriminatory laws resembled the right of petitioning government. Justice William Brennan in *NAACP v. Button* (1963) directly addressed petitioning, explaining that "litigation may well be the sole practicable avenue open to a minority to petition for redress of grievances" and "there is no longer any doubt that the First and Fourteenth Amendments protect certain forms of orderly group activity."[12] He referenced the 1958 *NAACP* decision but no incorporation cases.

Edwards v. South Carolina (1963)

In its 8-1 *Edwards* decision, the Court applied the right of petitioning government to the state level. The background of the case involved a peaceful gathering of people on the state capitol grounds to express their grievances to government. Local officials arrested and sentenced them with fines and jail time for breach of the peace. Justice Potter Stewart reasoned that the state arrests, prosecutions, and punishments of protestors for peacefully petitioning their government "infringed the petitioners' constitutionally protected rights of free speech, free assembly, and freedom to petition for redress of their grievances."[13]

10 *Thomas v. Collins*, 323 U.S. 516, at 530, see also 539 (1945) (citation information omitted).

11 *NAACP v. Alabama ex rel. Patterson,* 357 U.S. 449, at 460 (1958) (citing *De Jonge,* 299 U.S. 353, at 364; *Thomas*, 323 U.S. 516, at 530; and *Gitlow v. People of New York,* 268 U.S. 652 (1925)).

12 *NAACP v. Button,* 371 U.S. 415, at 430 (1963).

13 *Edwards*, 372 U.S. 229, at 235.

He appealed to the well-established rationale that the Fourteenth Amendment protects fundamental rights at the state level. Stewart elaborated that "[i]t has long been established that these First Amendment freedoms are protected by the Fourteenth Amendment from invasion by the States" and credited *Gitlow*, *De Jonge*, and *Cantwell v. Connecticut* (1940) among the cases contributing to this development.[14] Stewart did not appeal directly to the Due Process Clause—although several of the decisions he cited had done so—nor did he reference the NAACP association cases. Toward the end of the opinion, he presented a quote from *Stromberg v. California* (1931) in which the Court argued that the Fourteenth Amendment protected "free political discussion to the end that government may be responsive to the will of the people and that changes may be obtained by lawful means" because this is "a fundamental principle of our constitutional system."[15]

For Stewart, the context of the case demonstrated that the right of petitioning government was at its core. As he elaborated, the petitioners were "peaceably assembled at the site of the State Government and there peaceably expressed their grievances 'to the citizens of South Carolina, along with the Legislative Bodies of South Carolina.'"[16] This was an example of petitioning government, overlapping as it did in this situation with speech and assembly. Stewart occasionally used "peaceful expression" to refer to the group activity that was focused on petitioning government. As he declared, "[t]he Fourteenth Amendment does not permit a State to make criminal the peaceful expression of unpopular views."[17]

Confirmation

Following *Edwards*, the Court has recognized petitioning government as an incorporated right; however, it has been somewhat ambiguous about the incorporation case. For example, Justice Hugo Black in *Gideon v. Wainwright* (1963) explained that among the federal rights that the Court "made immune from state invasion by the Fourteenth, or some part of it, are the First Amendment's freedoms of speech, press, religion, assembly, association, and petition for redress of grievances."[18] He referenced *Edwards* as the case in which the Court incorporated not just petition,

14 Ibid. (citing among other cases, *Gitlow*, 268 U.S. 652 (1925); *De Jonge*, 299 U.S. 353; and *Cantwell v. Connecticut*, 310 U.S. 296 (1940)).

15 *Edwards*, 372 U.S. 229, at 238 (quoting *Stromberg v. California*, 283 U.S. 359, at 369 (1931)).

16 *Edwards*, 372 U.S. 229, at 235.

17 Ibid., at 237.

18 *Gideon v. Wainwright*, 372 U.S. 335, at 341 (1963).

but also speech and assembly.[19] The Court in *Henry v. Rock Hill* (1964) affirmed that "*Edwards* established that the 'Fourteenth Amendment does not permit a State to make criminal the peaceful expression of unpopular views'" but did not clarify that this related to petitioning government.[20] In *Brotherhood of Railroad Trainmen v. Virginia* (1964), a case about association, Black stated more than once that the First Amendment rights of speech, assembly, and petition applied at the state level yet did not cite any incorporation cases.[21] Justice John Paul Stevens in *NAACP v. Claiborne Hardware* (1982) stated that "[i]n *Edwards v. South Carolina,* we held that a peaceful march and demonstration was protected by the rights of free speech, free assembly, and freedom to petition for a redress of grievances."[22]

Justices have given clearer verifications that the Court in *Edwards* extended the petitioning right to the state level. Black explained in *Cox v. Louisiana* (1965) that the *Edwards* majority held that under the Constitution, "South Carolina could not punish people for assembling at the capitol to petition for redress of grievances."[23] In his dissent of *Adderly v. Florida* (1966), Justice William Douglas stated that "[t]he First Amendment, applicable to the States by reason of the Fourteenth (*Edwards v. South Carolina*), provides that 'Congress shall make no law ... abridging ... the right of the people peaceably to assemble, and to petition the Government for a redress of grievances.'"[24] While this statement mentions assembly and petitioning, *Adderly* was about the right to petition government.

The imprecise nature of Court statements about *Edwards* as the petition incorporation case is likely because justices occasionally describe political activities with terms that the Bill of Rights does not use, like association, expression, picket, and protest. They have also sometimes simply included petitioning along with other rights. As Brennan mentioned in his *McDonald v. Smith* (1985) concurrence, "we have recurrently treated the right to petition similarly to, and frequently as overlapping with, the First Amendment's other guarantees of free expression."[25]

19 Ibid., at 341–42 n. 4.

20 *Henry v. City of Rock Hill*, 376 U.S. 776, at 778 (1964) (*per curiam*; quoting *Edwards*, 372 U.S. 229, at 237).

21 *Brotherhood of Railroad Trainmen v. Virginia ex rel. Virginia State Bar*, 377 U.S. 1, at 2, 5 (1964).

22 *NAACP v. Claiborne Hardware Co.*, 458 U.S. 886, at 909 (1982) (citation information omitted).

23 *Cox v. Louisiana*, 379 U.S. 559, at 579 (1965).

24 *Adderly v. Florida*, 385 U.S. 39, at 48 (1966) (Douglas, W., dissenting; ellipses in original; citation information omitted).

25 *McDonald v. Smith*, 472 U.S. 479, at 490 (1985) (Brennan, W., concurring).

Summary

The *Edwards* majority incorporated the First Amendment right to petition government. The Court addressed the guarantee along with the previously incorporated rights of speech and assembly and reviewed the context of the case, which concerned petitioning government for redress of grievances. Stewart's statement that "South Carolina infringed the petitioners' constitutionally protected rights of free speech, free assembly, and freedom to petition for redress of their grievances," left little doubt that the Court considered petitioning as incorporated.[26] Yet, it has rarely credited *Edwards* as the incorporation case for this right.

26 *Edwards*, 372 U.S. 229, at 235.

PART II

SECOND AMENDMENT

Keep and Bear Arms

> "A well regulated Militia, being necessary to the security of a free State, the right of the people to keep and bear Arms, shall not be infringed."

The Second Amendment enumerates the right to keep and bear arms, which it specifically refers to as a "right of the people." The Supreme Court has regarded "keep" and "bear" together, as one right.[1] Unlike other federal rights, this one comes with a brief explanation. The reason for protecting firearm possession and use is to ensure that the nation's militia is at the ready. The Constitution authorizes Congress to call up a militia when needed to provide for order or security of the "State," which justices have read as meaning the federal government.[2] The Court incorporated the Second Amendment right in *McDonald v. Chicago* (2010) but appealed to a different justification.[3]

1 See *District of Columbia v. Heller*, 554 U.S. 570, at 646 (2008) (Stevens, J., dissenting).
2 See *Presser v. Illinois*, 116 U.S. 252, at 261–62 (1886); *Heller*, 554 U.S. 570, at 640–44 (Stevens, J., dissenting); and U.S. Constitution, Article I, Section 8.
3 *McDonald v. City of Chicago*, 561 U.S. 742 (2010).

Before *McDonald*

In one of its first considerations of the Second Amendment, in *United States v. Cruikshank* (1876), the Court followed its *Barron v. Baltimore* (1833) interpretation and held that, like all Bill of Rights' provisions, this right only applied against the federal government.[4] As Justice Morrison Waite in *Cruikshank* explained, regarding "bearing arms for a lawful purpose,"

> [t]he second amendment declares that it shall not be infringed; but this, as has been seen, means no more than that it shall not be infringed by Congress. This is one of the amendments that has no other effect than to restrict the powers of the national government.[5]

He added that local and state governments may justifiably protect and regulate gun ownership as an exercise of their police powers.[6]

The Court affirmed its *Cruikshank* view of the Second Amendment while elaborating the constitutional reasoning for preventing the federal government from violating the right to keep and bear arms in *Presser v. Illinois* (1886). Justice William Woods cited *Cruikshank* in support of the position that "the amendment is a limitation only upon the power of Congress and the National government, and not upon that of the States."[7] However, he added that "the States cannot, even laying the constitutional provision in question out of view, prohibit the people from keeping and bearing arms" because to do so would "deprive the United States of their rightful resource for maintaining the public security, and disable the people from performing their duty to the general government."[8] In other words, state governments should not interfere with gun ownership, not because it is a right, but because doing so would interfere with the nation's militias, in turn weakening government's ability to ensure order and security. The Court in *Maxwell v. Dow* (1900) affirmed the *Presser* view that, while the Second Amendment only restricted the federal government, states may not prevent armed citizens since they were necessary for the reserve military.[9]

4 *United States v. Cruikshank*, 92 U.S. 542, at 552–53 (1876) (citing *Barron ex rel. Tiernan v. City of Baltimore*, 32 U.S. (7 Pet.) 243, at 250 (1833)).

5 *Cruikshank*, 92 U.S. 542, at 553.

6 Ibid.

7 *Presser*, 116 U.S. 252, at 265.

8 Ibid.

9 *Maxwell v. Dow*, 176 U.S. 581, at 597 (1900) (citing *Presser*, 116 U.S. 252).

Justice Pierce Butler in *Hamilton v. Regents of California* (1934) argued that the Second Amendment supported a state requirement that all students take a military tactics class.[10] The reason, he elaborated, was that the amendment was about keeping men ready to serve in either federal or state militias.[11] Citing the Second Amendment, *Presser*, and other cases for support, Butler did not regard keep and bear arms as a right that people could exercise against their state governments.[12]

The *District of Columbia v. Heller* (2008) 5-4 majority opinion presented an alternative reading of the Second Amendment, moving it away from militias. Justice Antonin Scalia argued that the amendment concerned the people more than the militia, and "[w]e start therefore with a strong presumption that the Second Amendment right is exercised individually and belongs to all Americans."[13] This was to say that "the Second Amendment confers an individual right to keep and bear arms."[14] He referred to this as "the individual-rights interpretation."[15] From this, Scalia asserted that "the inherent right of self-defense has been central to the Second Amendment right."[16] He added, however, that "[l]ike most rights, the right secured by the Second Amendment is not unlimited."[17] The Court in *Heller* defended the right to keep and bear arms but this ruling only concerned the District of Columbia, not the states.[18]

McDonald v. Chicago (2010)

In another 5-4 decision, the Court in *McDonald* incorporated the Second Amendment right. This case involved residents challenging city ordinances that restricted gun ownership to such an extent that they effectively prevented individuals from owning handguns in their homes for self-defense. Justice Samuel Alito, authoring the majority opinion, acknowledged that the Court had not previously heard a case about extending the keep and bear firearms right to the states.[19]

10 *Hamilton v. Regents of University of California*, 293 U.S. 245 (1934).
11 Ibid., at 260.
12 Ibid., at 260–61.
13 *Heller*, 554 U.S. 570, at 581.
14 Ibid., at 622.
15 Ibid., at 620.
16 Ibid., at 628, see also 599.
17 Ibid., at 626.
18 Ibid., at 635.
19 *McDonald*, 561 U.S. 742, at 758–59.

Alito relied on the *Heller* premise that individual self-defense was the core of the Second Amendment, referring to it as a "basic" and "fundamental" right.[20] As he elaborated, "[s]elf-defense is a basic right, recognized by many legal systems from ancient times to the present day, and the *Heller* Court held that individual self-defense is 'the central component' of the Second Amendment right."[21]

Alito thoroughly reviewed the Court's development of due process incorporation theory and provided detailed lists of incorporated and unincorporated rights. He summarized that during the 1960s, "the Court began to hold that the Due Process Clause fully incorporates particular rights contained in the first eight Amendments."[22] It also settled, Alito continued, on the *Duncan v. Louisiana* (1968) "governing standard," which is "whether a particular Bill of Rights guarantee is fundamental to *our* scheme of ordered liberty and system of justice."[23] He explained that the Court was now asking

> whether the right to keep and bear arms is fundamental to *our* scheme of ordered liberty, *Duncan*, or as we have said in a related context, whether this right is "deeply rooted in this Nation's history and tradition," *Washington v. Glucksberg* (1997).[24]

In *Duncan*, Justice Byron White argued that incorporated rights were "fundamental to the American scheme of justice," which he clarified in a note as "necessary to an Anglo-American regime of ordered liberty."[25] In *Glucksberg*, Chief Justice William Rehnquist referenced *Snyder v. Massachusetts* (1934) and *Palko v. Connecticut* (1937) for contributing to the due process defense of rights that are "deeply rooted in this Nation's history and tradition" and "implicit in the concept of ordered liberty."[26] Now, in *McDonald*, Alito held that "a provision of the Bill of Rights that protects a right that is fundamental from an American perspective applies equally to the Federal Government and the States. See *Duncan*."[27]

He ruled in no uncertain terms that "[w]e therefore hold that the Due Process Clause of the Fourteenth Amendment incorporates the Second Amendment right recognized in *Heller*."[28] For the Court in *McDonald*, because self-defense is a

20 Ibid., at 767, 791.

21 Ibid., at 767 (emphasis in original).

22 Ibid., at 763.

23 Ibid., at 764 (emphasis in original; citing *Duncan v. Louisiana*, 391 U.S. 145, at 149 n. 14 (1968)).

24 *McDonald*, 561 U.S. 742, at 767 (emphasis in original; citation information omitted; citing *Duncan*, 391 U.S. 145, at 149; and *Washington v. Glucksberg*, 521 U.S. 702, at 721 (1997)).

25 *Duncan*, 391 U.S. 145, at 149, 149–50 n. 14.

26 *Glucksberg*, 521 U.S. 702, at 721 (citing *Snyder v. Massachusetts*, 291 U.S. 97, at 105 (1934); and *Palko v. Connecticut*, 302 U.S. 319, at 325, 326 (1937)).

27 *McDonald*, 561 U.S. 742, at 791.

28 Ibid.

fundamental right and central to the Second Amendment, the Due Process Clause protects the civil liberty to keep and bear arms from state infringement.

Confirmation

The Court has acknowledged that it incorporated the right to keep and bear arms in *McDonald.* Justice Clarence Thomas suggested in *New York State Rifle & Pistol Association v. Bruen* (2022) that the Court protected the right against states in both *Heller* and *McDonald*; however, he has elsewhere pointed to *McDonald* as the incorporation case.[29]

In *Friedman v. Highland Park* (2015), Thomas stated at the outset that "in *McDonald*, we recognized that the Second Amendment applies fully against the States as well as the Federal Government."[30] He again affirmed this development in his *Silvester v. Becerra* (2018) dissent, writing that "[t]he Second Amendment protects 'the right of the people to keep and bear arms,' and the Fourteenth Amendment requires the States to respect that right, *McDonald v. Chicago* (2010)."[31] In the short unsigned *Caetano v. Massachusetts* (2016) opinion, the Court emphasized "that this 'Second Amendment right is fully applicable to the States,' *McDonald v. Chicago* (2010)."[32] Alito in his *Ramos v. Louisiana* (2020) dissent explained that among the "provisions of the Bill of Rights [that] apply with full force to the States, see [...] *McDonald* (Second Amendment)."[33]

Summary

In *McDonald*, the Court incorporated the Second Amendment right to keep and bear arms. As Alito succinctly stated in the opinion, we "hold that the Due Process Clause of the Fourteenth Amendment incorporates the Second Amendment right."[34] The Court has since confirmed that it extended the right to keep and bear firearms to the states in *McDonald.*

29 *New York State Rifle & Pistol Association v. Bruen*, 97 U.S. ___, at 8 (2022).

30 *Friedman v. City of Highland Park, Illinois*, 577 S. Ct. 1039, at 1039 (2015) (Thomas C., dissenting; citation information omitted).

31 *Silvester v. Xavier Becerra*, 583 U.S. ___, at 1 (2018) (Thomas, C., dissenting; citation information omitted).

32 *Caetano v. Massachusetts*, 577 S. Ct. 411, at 411 (2016) (*per curiam*; citation information omitted).

33 *Ramos v. Louisiana*, 590 U.S. ___, at 19 (2020) (Alito, S., dissenting; citation information omitted).

34 *McDonald*, 561 U.S. 742, at 791.

PART III

THIRD AMENDMENT

Quartering Soldiers

> "No Soldier shall, in time of peace be quartered in any house, without the consent of the Owner, nor in time of war, but in a manner to be prescribed by law."

Unlike most other federal rights, the Bill of Rights specifies some caveats to the Third Amendment protection against quartering soldiers in private homes and does not refer to it as a "right." The Supreme Court has not heard a case about government housing soldiers in homes and therefore has not considered if the guarantee applies to the state level. However, a federal appeals court in *Engblom v. Carey* (2d Cir. 1982) ruled in favor of incorporating the right.[1]

Before *Engblom*

Over the years, a few justices have appeared supportive of extending the federal protection against housing soldiers to the state level and some lower court judges have asserted that it was a "fundamental right," thereby restricting state governments. Justice William Douglas in his *Poe v. Ullman* (1961) dissent reasoned, "[c]an there be any doubt that a Bill of Rights that in time of peace bars soldiers from being

1 *Engblom v. Carey*, 677 F.2d 957 (2d Cir. 1982).

quartered in a home 'without the consent of the Owner' should also bar the police from investigating the intimacies of the marriage relation?"[2] Justice John Harlan II in his *Poe* dissent argued that the Third and Fourth Amendments contributed to protecting "privacy in the home."[3] Douglas and Harlan used the *Palko v. Connecticut* (1937) concepts of "shocking" and "scheme of ordered liberty."[4] Douglas elaborated that a government may impinge upon rights "so long as what it does fails to shock the sensibilities of a majority of the Court."[5] For Harlan, "the concept of 'privacy' embodied in the Fourth Amendment is part of the 'ordered liberty' assured against state action by the Fourteenth Amendment."[6]

Authoring the *Griswold v. Connecticut* (1965) opinion, Douglas again associated the Third Amendment with the right of privacy, arguing that the shadows it and some other enumerated rights cast overlapped to create the right of privacy.[7] This suggested that the Third Amendment could prohibit state governments from quartering soldiers in homes, but Douglas did not defend the right as applicable to the states. While a few justices have since mentioned the discussion in *Griswold* about the Third Amendment, none have claimed the decision incorporated the right.[8] Harlan in his *Griswold* concurrence argued that the Court should follow the *Palko* "ordered liberty" approach to evaluate state-level violations of civil liberties.[9]

In the Southern District of New York Court decision of *Engblom v. Carey* (S.D. N.Y. 1981), Judge Robert Sweet regarded the Third Amendment guarantee as incorporated. The plaintiffs of the case argued that the state eviction of striking correctional officers from their on-site subsidized residencies to house National Guard members violated their Third Amendment right. Quoting *Palko* and *Griswold*, Sweet argued that the protection against quartering soldiers was, "[u]nder any of the theories extant, perhaps most likely as a right 'so rooted in the tradition and conscience of our people as to be ranked as fundamental' and thus 'implicit in the concept of ordered liberty.'"[10] As a fundamental right of America's ordered liberty, "the right not to have troops quartered in one's home must be considered so incorporated."[11] However, Sweet ruled that the state did not violate

2 *Poe v. Ullman*, 367 U.S. 497, at 522 (1961) (Douglas, W., dissenting).
3 Ibid., at 549 (Harlan, J., dissenting).
4 *Palko v. Connecticut*, 302 U.S. 319, at 325, 328 (1937).
5 *Poe*, 367 U.S. 497, at 518 (Douglas, J., dissenting).
6 Ibid., at 549 (Harlan, J., dissenting).
7 *Griswold v. Connecticut*, 381 U.S. 479, at 484–85 (1965).
8 See, for example, *Katz v. United States*, 389 U.S. 347, at 350 n. 5 (1967).
9 *Griswold*, 381 U.S. 479, at 500 (Harlan, J. concurring) (citing *Palko*, 302 U.S. 319, at 325).
10 *Engblom v. Carey*, 522 F. Supp. 57, at 65 (S.D. N.Y. 1981) (quoting *Palko*, 302 U.S. 319, at 325; and *Griswold*, 381 U.S. 479, at 500 (Harlan, J. concurring)).
11 *Engblom*, 522 F. Supp. 57, at 65.

this right since the correctional officers' occupancy of the government property was "most analogous to possession incident to employment."[12] The housing came with their jobs and, while state laws might offer protection, the Fourteenth and Third Amendments were not relevant in this situation.

Engblom v. Carey (2d. Cir. 1982)

The Second Circuit Court of Appeals in *Engblom* agreed with the District Court that the Fourteenth Amendment incorporated the Third Amendment prohibition against housing soldiers in private homes. It also reversed the lower court's ruling that the state did not violate this right.[13] According to the Appeals Court, other than the District Court that first heard the case, this was the first time that a federal court directly addressed the issue of whether the Third Amendment protected people from state governments.[14]

Appeals Court Judge Walter Mansfield reviewed the lower court's holding "that the Third Amendment is incorporated into the Fourteenth Amendment since it is one of the 'fundamental' rights 'rooted in the tradition and conscience of our people' and thus 'implicit in the concept of ordered liberty.'"[15] Like Sweet, he quoted passages from *Palko* and Harlan's concurring *Griswold* opinion. Mansfield held that "we agree with the district court that the Third Amendment is incorporated into the Fourteenth Amendment for application to the states."[16] After all, "[t]he Third Amendment was designed to assure a fundamental right to privacy."[17] For support, he referenced *Griswold* and the *Poe* dissenting opinions, all of which mentioned that the Third Amendment helped protect privacy.[18]

As with Fourth Amendment privacy guarantees, Mansfield reasoned that a person did not have to legally own a residence; occupancy or use was sufficient to exercise the Third Amendment.[19] Otherwise, an apartment tenant could be "denied a privacy right against the forced quartering of troops."[20] He ruled that

12 Ibid., at 67.
13 *Engblom*, 677 F.2d 957, at 961.
14 Ibid., at 959.
15 Ibid., at 961 (quoting *Griswold*, 381 U.S. 479, at 500 (Harlan, J., concurring); and *Palko*, 302 U.S. 319, at 325).
16 *Engblom*, 677 F.2d 957, at 961.
17 Ibid., at 962.
18 *Griswold*, 381 U.S. 479, at 484; and *Poe*, 367 U.S. 497, at 522 (Douglas, J., dissenting); 549 (Harlan, J., dissenting).
19 *Engblom*, 677 F.2d 957, at 962.
20 Ibid.

the appellants' interest in their quarters "reasonably entitled them to a legitimate expectation of privacy protected by the Third Amendment" and therefore "we reverse the summary dismissal of their Third Amendment claim."[21]

Judge Irving Kaufman in his partial dissent agreed with the court's protection of the right at the state level. The guarantee against housing soldiers in private residences during peacetime, he explained, "embraces aspects of liberty and privacy that have justified the application of the Fourth Amendment's prohibition against unreasonable searches and seizures to the states."[22] Kaufman affirmed that "Judge Sweet properly concluded that the Third Amendment is incorporated into the Due Process Clause of the Fourteenth Amendment."[23]

Confirmation

Two lower federal courts regard the Third Amendment as incorporated. However, courts outside of a federal appeals court jurisdiction do not have to follow its decisions. Moreover, the Court has prohibited federal courts from overruling its existing precedents.[24] On this last point, Judge Richard Wesley in *Bach v. Pataki* (2d Cir. 2005) elaborated that a lower federal court may not "incorporate rights in the absence of a Supreme Court precedent doing so."[25]

Yet, some lower federal courts have confirmed the 1982 *Engblom* holding that the Due Process Clause incorporates the Third Amendment guarantee against housing soldiers in private homes.[26] Upon return to the Southern District Court, for example, Sweet confirmed that "[t]he Court of Appeals also agreed that the Third Amendment is incorporated into the Fourteenth Amendment for application to the states."[27] For federal judges, other than the 1982 *Engblom* decision, "[j]udicial interpretation of the Third Amendment is nearly nonexistent."[28] The

21 Ibid., at 963, 964.

22 Ibid., at 967 (Kaufman, I., partial dissenting).

23 Ibid., at 968.

24 See *Rodriguez de Quijas v. Shearson/American Express, Inc.,* 490 U.S. 477, at 484 (1989); and *Agostini v. Felton,* 521 U.S. 203, at 237; 258 (Ginsburg, R., dissenting) (1997).

25 *Bach v. Pataki*, 408 F.3d 75, at 86 n. 24 (2d Cir. 2005).

26 See, for example, *SFF-Tir, LLC v. Stephenson*, 262 F. Supp. 3d 1165, at 1231 n. 78 (N.D. Okla. 2017); *Custer County Action Ass'n v. Garvey*, 256 F.3d 1024, at 1043 (10th Cir. 2001); and *United States v. Basurto*, 117 F. Supp. 3d 1266, at 1287 n. 6 (D. N.M. 2015).

27 *Engblom v. Carey*, 572 F. Supp. 44, at 46 (S.D. N.Y. 1983).

28 *Custer*, 256 F.3d 1024, at 1043.

Court has not had the opportunity to decide whether the right of no quartering of soldiers extends to the state level.

In a *McDonald v. Chicago* (2010) note, Justice Samuel Alito verified that among unincorporated rights was "the Third Amendment's protection against quartering of soldiers."[29] He elaborated that the *Engblom* decision of 1982 was a "holding as a matter of first impression that the 'Third Amendment is incorporated into the Fourteenth Amendment for application to the states.'"[30]

Summary

Lower federal courts have "as a matter of first impression" incorporated the right prohibiting government housing of soldiers in a private home without the owner's consent, as Alito confirmed, but the Court has not had the opportunity to rule on this matter. The Court's appeal to the Third Amendment when developing the unenumerated right of privacy in *Poe* and *Griswold* indicates that it might be receptive to applying the right against quartering soldiers to the state level.

29 *McDonald v. City of Chicago*, 561 U.S. 742, at 765 n. 13 (2010).
30 Ibid. (citing *Engblom*, 677 F.2d 957, at 961).

PART IV

FOURTH AMENDMENT

Unreasonable Searches and Seizures

> "The right of the people to be secure in their persons, houses, papers, and effects, against unreasonable searches and seizures, shall not be violated."

The Supreme Court in *Wolf v. Colorado* (1949) held that the Fourth Amendment "right of the people" to be free from "unreasonable searches and seizures" applied to the state level.[1] The Court has defined "unreasonable searches and seizures" as "arbitrary intrusion by the police," a phrase it has sometimes used in place of the specific constitutional wording.[2] Justices have also referred to this guarantee as the "Fourth Amendment right of privacy."[3]

Before *Wolf*

Prior to *Wolf*, the Court defended reasonable searches and seizures as a federal right yet provided some basic reasons for protecting it from state governments. In *Boyd v. United States* (1886), Justice Joseph Bradley argued that it was unconstitutional

1 *Wolf v. Colorado*, 338 U.S. 25, at 27 (1949).
2 See, for example, ibid., at 27, 28.
3 See, for example, *Elkins v. United States*, 364 U.S. 206, at 222 (1960); *Mapp v. Ohio*, 367 U.S. 643, at 655 (1961); and *Katz v. United States*, 389 U.S. 347, at 350–51 (1967).

for the federal government to invade an innocent person's property because doing so violated the "indefeasible right of personal security, personal liberty and private property."[4] *Weeks v. United States* (1914) concerned the exclusionary rule at the federal level, but it also addressed unreasonable searches and seizures. Justice William Day explained that the Fourth Amendment placed "the courts of the United States and Federal officials, in the exercise of their power and authority, under limitations and restraints."[5] The reason for this check on the abuse of government power is "to forever secure the people, their persons, houses, papers and effects, against all unreasonable searches and seizures under the guise of law."[6]

The Court incorporated a few Bill of Rights' protections in the early twentieth century, including some First and Sixth Amendment rights. For most of these rulings, it reasoned that the Fourteenth Amendment due process protection of liberty included fundamental rights. It developed this rationale in various cases including *Hurtado v. California* (1884), *Twining v. New Jersey* (1908), and *Gitlow v. New York* (1925).[7]

However, Justice Benjamin Cardozo presented an alternative incorporation approach in *Snyder v. Massachusetts* (1934) and *Palko v. Connecticut* (1937). In both *Snyder* and *Palko*, he argued that the Due Process Clause only protected federal rights against state violations of a "principle of justice so rooted in the traditions and conscience of our people as to be ranked as fundamental."[8] In *Palko*, Cardozo clarified that such fundamental principles were the nation's "very essence of a scheme of ordered liberty."[9] These included the few Bill of Rights' protections that the Court had already incorporated. However, he asserted that most trial protections were not fundamental. In *Snyder*, Cardozo explained that "[d]ue process of law requires that the proceedings shall be fair, but fairness is a relative, not an absolute, concept. It is fairness with reference to particular conditions or particular results."[10] Examples of such malleable justice procedures, he elaborated in *Palko*, included federal protections of grand jury indictment, jury trial, and no

4 *Boyd v. United States*, 116 U.S. 616, at 630 (1886).
5 *Weeks v. United States*, 232 U.S. 383, at 391–92 (1914).
6 Ibid., at 392.
7 *Hurtado v. People of California*, 110 U.S. 516, at 541 (1884) (Harlan, J. dissenting); *Twining v. State of New Jersey*, 211 U.S. 78, at 99, 106 (1908); and *Gitlow v. People of New York*, 268 U.S. 652, at 666 (1925).
8 *Snyder v. Massachusetts*, 291 U.S. 97, at 105 (1934); and *Palko v. Connecticut*, 302 U.S. 319, at 325 (1937) (quoting *Snyder*, 291 U.S. 97, at 105).
9 *Palko*, 302 U.S. 319, at 325.
10 *Snyder*, 291 U.S. 97, at 116.

self-incrimination, each of which states could modify or eliminate without denying due process of law.[11]

Wolf v. Colorado (1949)

Although the issue before the Court in *Wolf* was state admission of illegally obtained evidence in a criminal prosecution, it extended the Fourth Amendment right against unreasonable searches and seizures to the state level. Without elaborating the background of the case, Justice Felix Frankfurter in the 6-3 majority opinion asked whether the evidence collected was done through a search and seizure that was, following *Weeks*, unreasonable.[12]

Frankfurter wove his due process defense of basic rights into the protection of reasonable searches and seizures from state infringement. He asserted that he was following the *Palko* ordered liberty approach.[13] In part, he explained, this meant that the Court should consider the individual rights of the first eight amendments for application to the states one at a time, rather than assume "that the Due Process Clause incorporated the original Bill of Rights" all at once.[14] It also meant that, while there were fundamental rights, they were subject to change. For Frankfurter, due process "is the compendious expression for all those rights which the courts must enforce because they are basic to our free society. But basic rights do not become petrified as of any one time."[15] Society may consider some rights as universal, yet it may also mold others to better fit changing values. "Representing as it does a living principle," Frankfurter elaborated, "due process is not confined within a permanent catalogue of what may at a given time be deemed the limits or the essentials of fundamental rights."[16] He did not reference the recent cases of *Everson v. Board of Education* (1947), *Cole v. Arkansas* (1948), and *In re Oliver* (1948) in which the same Court respectively incorporated the First Amendment protection against government establishment of religion and Sixth Amendment guarantees that criminal defendants be informed of accusations and have public trials.[17]

11 *Palko*, 302 U.S. 319, at 323–24.
12 *Wolf*, 338 U.S. 25, at 25–26.
13 Ibid., at 26.
14 Ibid.
15 Ibid., at 27.
16 Ibid.
17 *Everson v. Board of Education of the Township of Ewing*, 330 U.S. 1 (1947); *Cole v. Arkansas*, 333 U.S. 196 (1948); and *In re Oliver*, 333 U.S. 257 (1948).

Due process in the United States currently included the fundamental right to reasonable searches and seizures, a guarantee that Frankfurter also referred to as the right against "arbitrary intrusion."[18] He ruled that

> [t]he security of one's privacy against arbitrary intrusion by the police—which is at the core of the Fourth Amendment—is basic to a free society. It is therefore implicit in "the concept of ordered liberty" and as such enforceable against the States through the Due Process Clause.[19]

Lawful searches and seizures protected a person's privacy against "[t]he knock at the door, whether by day or by night, as a prelude to a search, without authority of law but solely on the authority of the police."[20] He reiterated that "we have no hesitation in saying that were a State affirmatively to sanction such police incursion into privacy it would run counter to the guaranty of the Fourteenth Amendment."[21] The nation's "ordered liberty" determined that reasonable searches and seizures was a fundamental right, according to Frankfurter, and therefore the Due Process Clause protected it against state violation.

All the justices regarded lawful searches and seizures as a right existing at both state and federal levels of government. Justice Hugo Black in his concurrence stated that "I agree with the conclusion of the Court that the Fourth Amendment's prohibition of 'unreasonable searches and seizures' is enforceable against the states."[22] Justice William Douglas and Justice Frank Murphy in their respective dissents also expressed support for the Court's extension of the right to the state level.[23]

As far as for the federal rule restricting the use of illegally collected evidence in a prosecution, however, the Court in *Wolf* held that it did not apply to the states. As Frankfurter stated, "in a prosecution in a State court for a State crime the Fourteenth Amendment does not forbid the admission of evidence obtained by an unreasonable search and seizure."[24] Frankfurter reasoned that the exclusionary rule was not an integral aspect of ordered liberty because states could provide other means of "deterring unreasonable searches."[25] Later, in *Mapp v. Ohio* (1961), the Court overturned its *Wolf* ruling that states may admit illegally collected evidence

18 *Wolf*, 338 U.S. 25, at 27, 28.
19 Ibid., 27–28 (quoting *Palko*, 302 U.S. 319, at 325).
20 *Wolf*, 338 U.S. 25, at 28.
21 Ibid.
22 Ibid., at 39 (Black, H., concurring).
23 Ibid., at 40 (Douglas, W., dissenting); 41 (Murphy, F., dissenting).
24 Ibid., at 33.
25 Ibid., at 31.

in trials but not its protection of the Fourth Amendment guarantee of reasonable searches and seizures.[26]

Confirmation

Since 1949, several justices have agreed that the Court in *Wolf* protected the right to reasonable searches and seizures against state governments. Initially, a few references listed *Wolf* along with other cases. Black in *Gideon v. Wainwright* (1963) and Justice William Brennan in *Malloy v. Hogan* (1964) each asserted that the Court incorporated this Fourth Amendment right in *Wolf*, *Elkins*, and *Mapp*.[27] Justice Arthur Goldberg in his *Pointer v. Texas* (1965) and *Griswold v. Connecticut* (1965) concurrences listed *Wolf* with other decisions, such as *Mapp*, but did not associate a specific right with each case.[28] The Court, it should be mentioned, regards *Mapp* as protecting the exclusionary rule, not the enumerated right against unreasonable searches and seizures.[29]

Aside from a few loose references, the Court has often confirmed *Wolf* as the decision in which it extended reasonable searches and seizures to the states. As Justice Charles Whittaker in his *Frank v. Maryland* (1959) concurrence stated, "[t]he core of the Fourth Amendment prohibiting unreasonable searches applies to the States through the Due Process Clause of the Fourteenth Amendment. *Wolf v. Colorado*."[30] Frankfurter in *Stefanelli v. Minard* (1951) and Douglas in his dissent of that case affirmed the same.[31] Other acknowledgments that *Wolf* is the reasonable search and seizure incorporation case include Justice Robert Jackson in *Irvine v. California* (1954), Justice Potter Stewart in *Elkins v. United States* (1960), Justice Tom Clark in *Mapp*, Justice John Harlan II in his *Ker v. California* (1963) concurrence, and Justice Samuel Alito in *McDonald v. Chicago* (2010).[32]

26 *Mapp*, 367 U.S. 643.

27 *Gideon v. Wainwright*, 372 U.S. 335, at 342 n. 6 (1963); and *Malloy v. Hogan*, 378 U.S. 1, at 6 n. 5 (1964).

28 *Pointer v. Texas*, 380 U.S. 400, at 412 n. 3 (1965) (Goldberg, A., concurring); and *Griswold v. Connecticut*, 381 U.S. 479, at 488 n. 2 (1965) (Goldberg, A., concurring).

29 See, for example, *Albright v. Oliver*, 510 U.S. 266, at 272–73 (1994); and *McDonald v. City of Chicago*, 561 U.S. 742, at 764 n. 12 (2010).

30 *Frank v. Maryland*, 359 U.S. 360, at 373 (1959) (Whittaker, C., concurring).

31 *Stefanelli v. Minard*, 342 U.S. 117, at 119–20; 125 (Douglas, W., dissenting) (1951).

32 *Irvine v. California*, 347 U.S. 128, at 137 (1954); *Elkins*, 364 U.S. 206, at 213; *Mapp*, 367 U.S. 643, at 654–55; *Ker v. California*, 374 U.S. 23, at 44–45 (1963) (Harlan, J., concurring); and *McDonald*, 561 U.S. 742, at 764 n. 12.

Summary

The Court in *Wolf* defended the Fourth Amendment right against unreasonable searches and seizures at the state level. As Frankfurter argued, this "basic" right is "implicit in 'the concept of ordered liberty' and as such enforceable against the States through the Due Process Clause."[33] The Court has since recognized that it incorporated this right in *Wolf*.

33 *Wolf*, 338 U.S. 25, at 27–28 (quoting *Palko*, 302 U.S. 319, at 325).

Valid Search Warrants

> "[N]o Warrants shall issue, but upon probable cause, supported by Oath or affirmation, and particularly describing the place to be searched, and the persons or things to be seized."

The Supreme Court incorporated the Fourth Amendment search warrant requirement in *Aguilar v. Texas* (1964).[1] It has approached this right as inclusive of "probable cause, supported by Oath or affirmation, and particularly describing the place to be searched, and the persons or things to be seized."[2] In other words, the Court does not regard these requirements of a valid search warrant as separate rights.

Before *Aguilar*

The Court in *Frank v. Maryland* (1959), *Mapp v. Ohio* (1961), and *Ker v. California* (1963) suggested that the warrant requirement could press upon the states. In

1 *Aguilar v. Texas*, 378 U.S. 108 (1964).

2 See, for example, *Weeks v. United States*, 232 U.S. 383, at 391 (1914); *Katz v. United States*, 389 U.S. 347, at 357 (1967); *Terry v. Ohio*, 392 U.S. 1, at 20–21 (1968); *Spinelli v. United States*, 393 U.S. 410, at 415, 419 (1969); *Illinois v. Gates*, 462 U.S. 213, at 235 (1983); and *Albright v. Oliver*, 510 U.S. 266, at 274 (1994).

Frank, Justice Felix Frankfurter explained that "evidence of criminal action may not, save in very limited and closely confined situations, be seized without a judicially issued search warrant."[3] However, he argued that states had "analogues" to the federal warrant guarantee, negating a reason for incorporating it into the Due Process Clause.[4]

In *Mapp*, the Court's framing of the Fourth Amendment as a protection against capricious police searches implied that the valid warrant right could apply at the state level. In its incorporation of reasonable searches and seizures in *Wolf v. Colorado* (1949), the Court appealed to "[t]he security of one's privacy against arbitrary intrusion by the police—which is at the core of the Fourth Amendment."[5] While *Mapp* concerned the exclusionary rule, because the case involved a search warrant that police later failed to produce in court, it too appealed to a similar broad protection, namely, "the right to privacy free from unreasonable state intrusion."[6]

Ker was about local officers seizing marijuana from suspects without a warrant, which the Court agreed was admissible evidence if probable cause or incident to arrest informed the search.[7] The Court in *Ker* reiterated its Fourteenth Amendment Due Process Clause protection of fundamental rights, albeit in reference to reasonable searches and seizures.[8] Referring to this right, Justice Tom Clark argued "[t]hat safeguard has been declared to be 'as of the very essence of constitutional liberty' the guaranty of which 'is as important and as imperative as are the guaranties of the other fundamental rights of the individual citizen.'"[9] As a fundamental right, the Fourteenth Amendment protected reasonable searches and seizures from state infringement, and "the standard of reasonableness is the same under the Fourth and Fourteenth Amendments."[10] However, trial courts could adjust what constitutes reasonableness according to "the facts and circumstances of the case." The Court did not extend the warrant requirement to the state level in any of these decisions.

3 *Frank v. Maryland*, 359 U.S. 360, at 365 (1959).
4 Ibid. at 365–66.
5 *Wolf v. Colorado*, 338 U.S. 25, at 27–28 (1949).
6 *Mapp v. Ohio*, 367 U.S. 643, at 654 (1961).
7 *Ker v. California*, 374 U.S. 23, at 34–35, 38 (1963).
8 Ibid., at 31 n. 7, 32–34.
9 Ibid., at 32 (quoting *Gouled v. United States*, 255 U.S. 298, at 304 (1921)).
10 *Ker*, 374 U.S. 23, at 33.

Aguilar v. Texas (1964)

In addressing the necessities of a valid search warrant, the Court in its 6-3 *Aguilar* decision protected the Fourth Amendment warrant requirement from state abridgment. The case concerned "reliable information from a credible person" and city police officers' "belief" serving as the probable cause of a search warrant, rather than the informed and neutral deliberations of the issuing judge.[11]

Justice Arthur Goldberg referenced *Ker* to argue that the Fourth Amendment warrant requirement applied to the state level. He reviewed that "[i]n *Ker v. California*, we held that the Fourth 'Amendment's proscriptions are enforced against the States through the Fourteenth Amendment,' and that 'the standard of reasonableness is the same under the Fourth and Fourteenth Amendments.'"[12] Continuing, he reasoned that "[a]lthough *Ker* involved a search without a warrant, that case must certainly be read as holding that the standard for obtaining a search warrant is likewise 'the same under the Fourth and Fourteenth Amendments.'"[13] In other words, the Court made the incorporation defense applicable to the warrant requirement in *Ker* but, because that case did not involve a warrant whereas *Aguilar* did, *Aguilar* incorporated the right.

The Court in *Aguilar* also recommended a way to test the validity of state warrants. A valid warrant required police to inform a magistrate of the "underlying circumstances" in order to "provide a sufficient basis for a finding of probable cause."[14] Goldberg held that in this case, "the search warrant should not have been issued because the affidavit did not provide a sufficient basis for a finding of probable cause."[15] Regardless of these standards, the Court ruled that the Fourth Amendment warrant right was "fundamental" and therefore the Fourteenth Amendment protected it from state violation.

Confirmation

The Court considers the warrant requirement as incorporated yet rarely credits *Aguilar* for this development. Some justices have referenced *Aguilar* in broader discussions, such as Goldberg in *United States v. Ventresca* (1965), who mentioned

11 *Aguilar*, 378 U.S. 108, at 110, 114–16.
12 Ibid., 110 (citation information omitted; quoting *Ker*, 374 U.S. 23, at 33).
13 *Aguilar*, 378 U.S. 108, at 110.
14 Ibid., at 114–15.
15 Ibid., at 115.

the case several times in relation to valid warrants.[16] Justice John Harlan II in *Spinelli v. United States* (1969) explained that the "tests it establishes were designed to implement the long-standing principle that probable cause must be determined by a 'neutral and detached magistrate.'"[17] Justice William Rehnquist in *Franks v. Delaware* (1978) elaborated that the Court in *Aguilar* "held that the determination by a magistrate that the affidavit submitted to him made out 'probable cause' for purposes of the Fourth and Fourteenth Amendments was subject to later judicial review."[18] In *United States v. Leon* (1984), Justice Byron White included *Aguilar* along with *Ventresca* as cases in which the Court "expressed a strong preference for warrants."[19] The Court sometimes, as in *Terry v. Ohio* (1968), indirectly acknowledges *Aguilar* as the incorporation case by referencing it and other rulings in support of warrant requirements and exceptions.[20]

Along with the nuances involved with warrants, perhaps a reason that justices do not clearly cite *Aguilar* for incorporating the warrant requirement is because the Court later rejected that decision's validity test. In *Illinois v. Gates* (1983), Rehnquist explained that "we conclude that it is wiser to abandon the 'two-pronged test' established by our decisions in *Aguilar* and *Spinelli*. In its place we reaffirm the totality-of-the-circumstances analysis that traditionally has informed probable-cause determinations."[21]

However, Justice Samuel Alito in *McDonald v. Chicago* (2010) confirmed *Aguilar* as the warrant requirement incorporation case. There, in his extensive listing of incorporated rights, he stated that "[w]ith respect to the Fourth Amendment, see *Aguilar v. Texas* (1964) (warrant requirement)."[22]

Summary

The Court incorporated the Fourth Amendment valid warrant requirement in *Aguilar*. For Goldberg, "the standard for obtaining a search warrant is likewise 'the same under the Fourth and Fourteenth Amendments.'"[23] He made this ruling

16 *United States v. Ventresca*, 380 U.S. 102 (1965).

17 *Spinelli*, 393 U.S. 410, at 415 (quoting *Johnson v. United States*, 333 U.S. 10, at 14 (1948)).

18 *Franks v. Delaware*, 438 U.S. 154, at 184 (1978) (Rehnquist, W., dissenting; citation information omitted).

19 *United States v. Leon*, 468 U.S. 897, at 914 (1984).

20 *Terry*, 392 U.S. 1, at 21 n. 19; see also *Spinelli*, 393 U.S. 410, at 415; *Gates*, 462 U.S. 213, at 216–17, 227, 238, 239; and *Albright*, 510 U.S. 266, at 274.

21 *Gates*, 462 U.S. 213, at 238.

22 *McDonald v. City of Chicago*, 561 U.S. 742, at 764 n. 12 (2010) (citation information omitted).

23 *Aguilar*, 378 U.S. 108, at 110 (quoting *Ker*, 374 U.S. 23, at 33).

in reference to *Ker*, rather than as a direct statement. While many justices have regarded the Fourth Amendment warrant guarantee as holding sway at the state level, few have clearly recognized *Aguilar* as the incorporation case.

PART V

FIFTH AMENDMENT

Grand Jury

> "No person shall be held to answer for a capital, or otherwise infamous crime, unless on a presentment or indictment of a Grand Jury, except in cases arising in the land or naval forces, or in the Militia, when in actual service in time of War or public danger."

A grand jury reviews information to determine if sufficient reasons exist to bring charges against the accused. Like the Third Amendment protection against quartering solders in private homes, the Fifth Amendment grand jury indictment right for capital criminal prosecutions includes a few exceptions. The Supreme Court has ruled against extending the grand jury guarantee to the state level, making this decision in *Hurtado v. California* (1884).[1]

Before *Hurtado*

Before it addressed the Fifth Amendment grand jury right in *Hurtado*, the Court held that federal indictments in general must provide unambiguous descriptions of criminal charges to defendants. Justice Smith Thompson in *United States v. Mills* (1833) asserted that "in all cases the offense must be set forth with clearness,

1 *Hurtado v. People of California*, 110 U.S. 516 (1884).

and all necessary certainty, to apprise the accused of the crime with which he stands charged."[2] He described this as a "general rule" and did not appeal to the Constitution or Fifth Amendment. Similarly, Justice Nathan Clifford in *United States v. Cook* (1872) wrote that "it is universally true that no indictment is sufficient if it does not accurately and clearly allege all the ingredients of which the offense is composed."[3]

The Court also considered the indictment process at the state level. Justice Morrison Waite in *Kennard v. Louisiana* (1876) held that "[a] mere statement of the facts" was sufficient to meet constitutional due process of law standards.[4] Yet, he added that the Court had no authority to require states to provide statements of facts as part of their prosecution procedures.[5] In *United States v. Cruikshank* (1876), Waite further described that indictments based on detailed statements of the charges are "an elementary principle of criminal pleading."[6] He elaborated that "[t]he object of the indictment is, first, to furnish the accused with such a description of the charge against him as will enable him to make his defence, [...] and, second, to inform the court of the facts alleged."[7] Waite counseled that courts should protect this right, which is not "so granted or secured."[8] However, he adhered to the Court's *Slaughter-House Cases* (1873) view that state and national citizenship—and therefore rights—were distinct, meaning that the Bill of Rights did not relate to the state level.[9] Before 1884, the Court established that criminal proceedings throughout the nation should have indictments that at a minimum informed the accused of criminal charges.

Hurtado v. California (1884)

The Court in *Hurtado* ruled 7-1 that the Fifth Amendment grand jury right did not restrict state governments from using other ways of charging suspects. This case addressed California's Constitution and laws that allowed district attorney information rather than grand jury hearing indictments to determine whether to

2 *United States v. Mills*, 32 U.S. (7 Pet.) 138, at 142 (1833).
3 *United States v. Cook*, 84 U.S. (17 Wall.) 168, at 174 (1872).
4 *Kennard v. Louisiana ex rel. Morgan*, 92 U.S. 480, at 483 (1876).
5 Ibid., at 481.
6 *United States v. Cruikshank*, 92 U.S. 542, at 558 (1876).
7 Ibid.
8 Ibid., at 555, 559.
9 Ibid., at 549 (citing *Slaughter-House Cases*, 83 U.S. (16 Wall.) 36, at 74 (1873)).

proceed with criminal prosecutions, even for crimes that could result in the death penalty.

Justice Stanley Matthews, writing the *Hurtado* opinion, argued that the due process of law passage in the Fifth and Fourteenth Amendments carried the same meaning and therefore the guarantee in the latter did not bring to the states additional prosecution protections, such as grand jury hearings. In a thorough historical review of the concept in England and America, he described due process as lawful procedures that prevent the arbitrary abuse of government power.[10] Matthews asserted that "'due process of law' was not meant or intended to include, *ex vi termini*, the institution and procedure of a grand jury in any case."[11] According to him, if the authors of the Fourteenth Amendment wanted to apply the grand jury hearing right to the states, then they would have specifically written this guarantee into the amendment.[12]

Matthews also explained that governments throughout the United States were republican, by which he meant that they already followed due process of law, including determining sufficient reasons to prosecute someone. He insisted that while due process of law in the Fifth and Fourteenth Amendments had the same basic meaning, they referred to different levels of government. Due process of law in the Fifth Amendment "refers to that law of the land which derives its authority from the legislative powers conferred upon Congress by the Constitution of the United States," whereas in the Fourteenth Amendment, it "derives its authority from the inherent and reserved powers of the State, exerted within the limits of those fundamental principles of liberty and justice which lie at the base of all our civil and political institutions."[13] These principles included "the right of the people to make their own laws, and alter them at their pleasure."[14] If the people of a state wanted grand jury hearings as part of their legal procedures, then they could work through their legislature to institute them. If the people approved of public officers presenting information to establish reasons for prosecuting suspects, then that too adhered to due process.

For the Court, the Due Process Clause of the Fourteenth Amendment recognized that states could determine their own judicial procedures; it did not extend Fifth Amendment protections to the states. Matthews ruled that

10 *Hurtado*, 110 U.S. 516, at 527–34.
11 Ibid., at 534.
12 Ibid., at 535.
13 Ibid.
14 Ibid.

> we are unable to say that the substitution for a presentment or indictment by a grand jury of the proceeding by information, after examination and commitment by a magistrate, certifying to the probable guilt of the defendant, with the right on his part to the aid of counsel, and to the cross-examination of the witnesses produced for the prosecution, is not due process of law.[15]

As long as a state had a public official certifying probable cause, along with other criminal trial protections, then not having a grand jury hearing was constitutional. States did not have to provide grand jury hearing indictments, but they did need some kind of "preliminary proceeding" to establish cause for moving forward with a prosecution.

Confirmation

The Court has recognized and followed its *Hurtado* ruling against applying the Fifth Amendment grand jury right to the state level. As Justice William Moody in *Twining v. New Jersey* (1908) stated, the Fourteenth Amendment did not provide "the guarantee against prosecution, except by indictment of a grand jury, contained in the Fifth Amendment (*Hurtado v. California*)."[16]

Other justices who have acknowledged that the Court in *Hurtado* declined to protect the grand jury right at the state level include Justice George Shiras in *Hallinger v. Davis* (1892) and *Hodgson v. Vermont* (1897), Chief Justice Melville Fuller in *McNulty v. California* (1893), Justice Henry Brown in *Holden v. Hardy* (1898) and *Bolln v. Nebraska* (1900), Justice David Brewer in *Brown v. New Jersey* (1899), Justice Rufus Peckham in *Maxwell v. Dow* (1900), Chief Justice William Taft in *Gaines v. Washington* (1928), Justice Benjamin Cardozo in *Snyder v. Massachusetts* (1934) and *Palko v. Connecticut* (1937), Justice William Brennan in *Malloy v. Hogan* (1964), and Chief Justice William Rehnquist in *Albright v. Oliver* (1994).[17] Justice Samuel Alito in *McDonald v. Chicago* (2010) listed among unincorporated rights, "*Hurtado v. California* (1884) (due process does not require

15 Ibid., at 538.

16 *Twining v. State of New Jersey*, 211 U.S. 78, at 98 (1908) (citation information omitted).

17 *Hallinger v. Davis*, 146 U.S. 314, at 322 (1892); *Hodgson v. Vermont*, 168 U.S. 262, at 272 (1897); *McNulty v. California*, 149 U.S. 645, at 648 (1893); *Holden v. Hardy*, 169 U.S. 366, at 384 (1898); *Bolln v. Nebraska*, 176 U.S. 83, at 86 (1900); *Brown v. New Jersey*, 175 U.S. 172, at 175 (1899); *Maxwell v. Dow*, 176 U.S. 581, at 584–5 (1900); *Gaines v. Washington*, 277 U.S. 81, at 86 (1928); *Snyder v. Massachusetts*, 291 U.S. 97, at 105 (1934); *Palko v. Connecticut*, 302 U.S. 319, at 323 (1937); *Malloy v. Hogan*, 378 U.S. 1, at 4 n. 2 (1964); and *Albright v. Oliver*, 510 U.S. 266, at 272 (1994).

grand jury indictment)."[18] Several of these confirmations elaborated that the Court in *Hurtado* ruled that states may have some kind of information phase instead of grand jury indictments.

Summary

The Court has not incorporated the Fifth Amendment right to a grand jury hearing. As Matthews stated in *Hurtado*, "'due process of law' was not meant or intended to include, *ex vi termini*, the institution and procedure of a grand jury in any case."[19] For the Court, a public officer establishing information to bring charges, such as at a preliminary hearing, provides the same basic due process protection as a grand jury indictment. Several justices have referred to *Hurtado* as the case in which the Court ruled against extending the grand jury right to the state level.

18 *McDonald v. City of Chicago*, 561 U.S. 742, at 759, see also 761 (2010) (citation information omitted).

19 *Hurtado*, 110 U.S. 516, at 534.

Double Jeopardy

> "No person shall [...] be subject for the same offence to be twice put in jeopardy of life or limb."

In *Benton v. Maryland* (1969), the Supreme Court incorporated the Fifth Amendment right to be free from double jeopardy.[1] This overturned the *Palko v. Connecticut* (1937) ruling that the Fourteenth Amendment did not prevent states from prosecuting a person more than once for the same crime.[2] The *Benton* majority also rejected the *Palko* incorporation approach.

Before *Benton*

Initially, the Court in *Palko* ruled 8-1 that the federal guarantee against double jeopardy did not apply to the states, arguing that it was not necessary for "ordered liberty." Justice Benjamin Cardozo explained that, for the Court, states had discretion over enforcing most trial rights. He gave the examples of the Court's refusal to impose on states the grand jury and self-incrimination guarantees of the Fifth

1 *Benton v. Maryland*, 395 U.S. 784 (1969).
2 *Palko v. Connecticut*, 302 U.S. 319 (1937).

Amendment. Cardozo elaborated that, regarding Sixth and Seventh Amendment protections, "[t]his court has ruled that consistently with those amendments trial by jury may be modified by a state or abolished altogether."[3] However, the Court would protect a federal right from state government violation if it was "of the very essence of a scheme of ordered liberty," which was to say, quoting his earlier *Snyder v. Massachusetts* (1934) opinion, "a 'principle of justice so rooted in the traditions and conscience of our people as to be ranked as fundamental.'"[4] According to Cardozo, referring mostly to incorporated First Amendment rights, "pledges of particular amendments have been found to be implicit in the concept of ordered liberty, and thus, through the Fourteenth Amendment, become valid as against the states."[5] In *Palko*, the Court did not favor protecting the double jeopardy prohibition at the state level because the state had not subjected the accused to "a hardship so acute and shocking that our polity will not endure it."[6] Justice Felix Frankfurter in *Wolf v. Colorado* (1949) made use of the *Palko* ordered liberty approach to defend the Fourth Amendment right against unreasonable searches and seizures at the state level.[7]

In other incorporation rulings since *Palko*, however, justices appealed to due process of law and fundamental rights rather than ordered liberty and rooted in traditions. In *Cantwell v. Connecticut* (1940), *In re Oliver* (1948), *Cole v. Arkansas* (1948), *Gideon v. Wainwright* (1963), and *Edwards v. South Carolina* (1963), the Court argued that the Due Process Clause of the Fourteenth Amendment protected fundamental rights at the state level.[8] In *Gideon*, for example, Justice Hugo Black argued that "those guarantees of the Bill of Rights which are fundamental safeguards of liberty immune from federal abridgment are equally protected against state invasion by the Due Process Clause of the Fourteenth Amendment."[9] The Court continued to use this due process incorporation rationale, adding in *Malloy v. Hogan* (1964) that states must protect incorporated rights with the "same standards" as the federal government.[10] A few justices around this time, prominently Justice John Harlan II, objected to this view.[11] Justices in

3 Ibid., at 324.

4 Ibid., at 325 (quoting *Snyder v. Massachusetts*, 291 U.S. 97, at 105 (1934)).

5 *Palko*, 302 U.S. 319, at 325.

6 Ibid., at 328.

7 *Wolf v. Colorado*, 338 U.S. 25, at 26 (1949).

8 *Cantwell v. Connecticut*, 310 U.S. 296, at 303 (1940); *In re Oliver*, 333 U.S. 257, at 273 (1948); *Cole v. Arkansas*, 333 U.S. 196, at 273 (1948); *Gideon v. Wainwright*, 372 U.S. 335, at 341 (1963); and *Edwards v. South Carolina*, 372 U.S. 229, at 235 (1963).

9 *Gideon*, 372 U.S. 335, at 341.

10 *Malloy v. Hogan*, 378 U.S. 1, at 10 (1964).

11 See, for example, ibid., at 15–17 (Harlan, J., dissenting).

other incorporation cases, including Chief Justice Earl Warren in *Washington v. Texas* (1967) and Justice Byron White in *Duncan v. Louisiana* (1968) adhered to the *Malloy* "same standards" view as they brought federal rights into the Due Process Clause.[12]

Benton v. Maryland (1969)

The Court in *Benton* focused on the Fifth Amendment right against double jeopardy in the context of the country's system of justice. In this case, a state retrial pronounced the defendant guilty of two charges, whereas an earlier trial had only found him guilty of just one of the offenses. The Court decided 6-2 that this was unconstitutional because the Due Process Clause protected the accused from double jeopardy. In ruling that this federal right now applied to the states, the Court in *Benton* rejected both the *Palko* holding and rationale.

Justice Thurgood Marshall explained that the Court would use the Due Process Clause defense of fundamental rights rather than the *Palko* approach.[13] In *Palko*, Cardozo considered the intensity of a government violation to determine whether the Fourteenth Amendment protected a federal right against states. Marshall described the Court's move away from this incorporation logic and toward one that considered whether state infringement of a Bill of Rights' "fundamental" guarantee denied due process of law. He referenced recent decisions, including *Gideon*, *Malloy*, and *Duncan*, as examples of the Court using this incorporation defense.[14] Marshall elaborated that in *Malloy*, the Court "rejected the notion that the Fourteenth Amendment applies to the States only a 'watered-down, subjective version of the individual guarantees of the Bill of Rights.'"[15] Now for the Court, "[o]nce it is decided that a particular Bill of Rights guarantee is 'fundamental to the American scheme of justice,' *Duncan v. Louisiana*, the same constitutional standards apply against both the State and Federal Governments."[16] Marshall summarized that "*Palko* represented an approach to basic constitutional rights which this Court's recent decisions have rejected."[17]

12 *Washington v. Texas*, 388 U.S. 14, at 18 (1967); and *Duncan v. Louisiana*, 391 U.S. 145, at 149 (1968).

13 *Benton*, 395 U.S. 784, at 794.

14 Ibid., at 794–95.

15 Ibid., at 794 (quoting *Malloy*, 378 U.S. 1, at 10–11).

16 *Benton*, 395 U.S. 784, at 795 (citation information omitted; quoting *Duncan*, 391 U.S. 145, at 149).

17 *Benton*, 395 U.S. 784, at 794.

Returning to double jeopardy, Marshall in *Benton* held that, just as the Court ruled in *Duncan* about the criminal jury trial right, freedom from being tried twice for the same criminal accusation "was 'fundamental to the American scheme of justice.'"[18] He asserted that "[t]he fundamental nature of the guarantee against double jeopardy can hardly be doubted."[19] Reviewing some history of the right, Marshall argued that the protection against double jeopardy "has from the very beginning been part of our constitutional tradition."[20] The Court defended the fundamental right against double jeopardy as part of the country's long-standing justice system, as well as its guarantee in the Bill of Rights. In the present case, the violation "must be judged, not by the watered-down standard enunciated in *Palko*, but under this Court's interpretations of the Fifth Amendment double jeopardy provision."[21] As a fundamental aspect of the nation's justice system, the right against double jeopardy existed at the state level with the same strength as at the national level. The Court ruled that "the double jeopardy prohibition of the Fifth Amendment represents a fundamental ideal in our constitutional heritage, and that it should apply to the States through the Fourteenth Amendment."[22] Marshall clarified that, "[i]nsofar as it is inconsistent with this holding, *Palko v. Connecticut* is overruled."[23]

Confirmation

The Court regards the right against double jeopardy as incorporated and many justices have recognized *Benton* for this development. In *North Carolina v. Pearce* (1969), which the Court announced along with *Benton*, Justice Potter Stewart explained that "[t]he Court has held today, in *Benton v. Maryland*, that the Fifth Amendment guarantee against double jeopardy is enforceable against the States through the Fourteenth Amendment."[24] Also in *Pearce*, Justice William Douglas in his concurrence and Harlan in his partial dissent acknowledged the same.[25] Stewart again confirmed *Benton* as applying the double jeopardy prohibition to the states in *Ashe v. Swenson* (1970) and *Crist v. Bretz* (1978).[26]

18 Ibid. (quoting *Duncan*, 391 U.S. 145, at 149).
19 *Benton*, 395 U.S. 784, at 795.
20 Ibid., at 796.
21 Ibid.
22 Ibid., at 794.
23 Ibid.
24 *North Carolina v. Pearce*, 395 U.S. 711, at 717 (1969) (citation information omitted).
25 *Pearce*, 395 U.S. 711, at 736 (Douglas, W., concurring); 744, 751 (Harlan, J., partial dissenting).
26 *Ashe v. Swenson*, 397 U.S. 436, at 437 (1970); and *Crist v. Bretz*, 437 U.S. 28, at 32 (1978).

Others verifying that the Court in *Benton* extended the Fifth Amendment freedom from double jeopardy to the state level include Chief Justice Warren Burger in *Waller v. Florida* (1970), Harlan in his *Ashe* concurrence, Justice William Rehnquist in *Robinson v. Neil* (1973), Justice William Brennan in his *Robinson* concurrence, Justice Harry Blackmun in *United States v. DiFrancesco* (1980), White in *Illinois v. Vitale* (1980), Marshall in *Heath v. Alabama* (1985), Rehnquist again, now as Chief Justice, in *Albright v. Oliver* (1994), and Justice Samuel Alito in *McDonald v. Chicago* (2010).[27]

Summary

The Court expressly incorporated the guarantee against double jeopardy in *Benton*. Marshall ruled that "the double jeopardy prohibition of the Fifth Amendment represents a fundamental ideal in our constitutional heritage, and that it should apply to the States through the Fourteenth Amendment."[28] Many justices have confirmed that the Court in *Benton* protected this right against state governments.

27 *Waller v. Florida*, 397 U.S. 387, at 390 (1970); *Ashe*, 397 U.S. 436, at 448 (Harlan, J., concurring); *Robinson v. Neil*, 409 U.S. 505, at 506, see also 510; 511 (Brennan, W., concurring) (1973); *United States v. DiFrancesco*, 449 U.S. 117, at 131 n. 12 (1980); *Illinois v. Vitale*, 447 U.S. 410, at 415 (1980); *Heath v. Alabama*, 474 U.S. 82, at 97 (1985) (Marshall, T. dissenting); *Albright v. Oliver*, 510 U.S. 266, at 273 (1994); and *McDonald v. City of Chicago*, 561 U.S. 742, at 764 n. 12 (2010).

28 *Benton*, 395 U.S. 784, at 794.

Self-Incrimination

> "No person shall [...] be compelled in any criminal case to be a witness against himself."

The Supreme Court in *Malloy v. Hogan* (1964) incorporated the Fifth Amendment right against compulsory self-incrimination.[1] In doing so, the Court overturned its earlier *Twining v. New Jersey* (1908) ruling that denied protecting the federal guarantee against states but not that decision's due process defense of fundamental rights.[2] *Malloy* is also noteworthy for establishing the "same standards" view of incorporated rights.

Before *Malloy*

The *Twining* 8-1 majority held that freedom from self-incrimination was neither a "privilege or immunity" nor essential for due process of law and therefore the federal right did not protect defendants at the state level.[3] However, the Court in *Twining* laid some of the groundwork of the due process protection of

1 *Malloy v. Hogan*, 378 U.S. 1 (1964).
2 *Twining v. State of New Jersey*, 211 U.S. 78 (1908).
3 Ibid., at 99, 107.

fundamental rights rationale that it would later use to incorporate several federal protections. Justice William Moody explained that the Court was investigating if "the exemption from self-incrimination is of such a nature that it must be included in the conception of due process. Is it a fundamental principle of liberty and justice which inheres in the very idea of free government?"[4] If a constitutional guarantee was fundamental to due process of law, then the Fourteenth Amendment would protect it against state transgression. For the Court in *Twining*, however, prevention of self-incrimination was not a fundamental right, it was a law.[5]

As late as *Adamson v. California* (1947), the Court upheld its *Twining* ruling that the Fifth Amendment prohibition of compelled self-incrimination did not extend to the state level. Justice Stanley Reed stated that, in agreement with *Twining*, "protection against self-incrimination is not a privilege or immunity of national citizenship."[6] While due process protected a "fair trial," he reasoned, "[t]he due process clause of the Fourteenth Amendment, however, does not draw all the rights of the federal Bill of Rights under its protection," as the Court held in *Palko v. Connecticut* (1937).[7]

Several cases addressing involuntary confessions since *Twining*, however, displayed a shift toward protecting the right against self-incrimination. Considering claims of officer threats and false promises as prompting a confession, the Court in *Lisenba v. California* (1941) argued that "[t]he aim of the requirement of due process is not to exclude presumptively false evidence, but to prevent fundamental unfairness in the use of evidence, whether true or false."[8] Putting it another way, the Court stated in *Rochin v. California* (1952)—a case in which the state gained evidence using a stomach pump—that "[c]oerced confessions offend the community's sense of fair play and decency."[9] It ruled against the admission of a confession made under threat in another state-level case, *Rogers v. Richmond* (1961), because "ours is an accusatorial and not an inquisitorial system—a system in which the State must establish guilt by evidence independently and freely secured and may not by coercion."[10]

Along with expanding its view of self-incrimination, the Court was using the Due Process Clause protection of fundamental rights rationale that it developed in a few cases including *Twining* and *Gitlow v. New York* (1925).[11] In *Palko*, however,

4 Ibid., at 106.
5 Ibid., at 113.
6 *Adamson v. California*, 332 U.S. 46, at 53 (1947).
7 Ibid. (citing *Palko v. Connecticut*, 302 U.S. 319, at 323 (1937)).
8 *Lisenba v. California*, 314 U.S. 219, at 236 (1941).
9 *Rochin v. California*, 342 U.S. 165, at 173 (1952).
10 *Rogers v. Richmond*, 365 U.S. 534, at 541 (1961).
11 *Twining*, 211 U.S. 78, at 106; and *Gitlow v. People of New York*, 268 U.S. 652, at 666 (1925).

Justice Benjamin Cardozo instead argued that the Court should only use the Due Process Clause to rule against state laws that were "acute and shocking" to "ordered liberty."[12] Most incorporation cases, however, continued to appeal to the due process of law protection of fundamental rights. As Justice Hugo Black in *Gideon v. Wainwright* (1963) explained, "this Court has looked to the fundamental nature of original Bill of Rights guarantees to decide whether the Fourteenth Amendment makes them obligatory on the States."[13]

Malloy v. Hogan (1964)

The Court incorporated the right against self-incrimination by a 5-4 vote in *Malloy*. The background of this case involved a defendant refusing to answer questions on the grounds that his responses might incriminate him, for which a county court held him in contempt. The Connecticut Supreme Court of Errors agreed with the lower court holding that the Fifth Amendment protection from self-incrimination was not available at the state level. The Court used the due process of law protection of fundamental rights reasoning to reverse the state and incorporate the right.

Justice William Brennan in the *Malloy* opinion appealed to the Due Process Clause defense of incorporation—describing it as "the view which has thus far prevailed"—and added to it.[14] He referenced *Chicago, Burlington & Quincy Railroad v. Chicago* (1897), *Twining*, and *Gitlow* as contributing to this rationale.[15] Brennan mentioned that the Court recently in *Gideon* "held that provision of counsel in all criminal cases was 'a fundamental right, essential to a fair trial,' and thus was made obligatory on the States by the Fourteenth Amendment."[16] As with that right, "[w]e hold today that the Fifth Amendment's exception from compulsory self-incrimination is also protected by the Fourteenth Amendment against abridgment by the States."[17]

In agreement with the appellants, Brennan explained that America's fundamental principles of due process of law were in place to establish an "accusatorial, not inquisitorial" criminal justice system.[18] Therefore, reiterating the Court's ruling,

12 *Palko*, 302 U.S. 319, at 328, 325.

13 *Gideon v. Wainwright*, 372 U.S. 335, at 341 (1963).

14 *Malloy*, 378 U.S. 1, at 4.

15 Ibid., at 4–5 (citing *Chicago, Burlington & Quincy Railroad Co. v. Chicago*, 166 U.S. 226 (1897); *Twining*, 211 U.S. 78, at 99; and *Gitlow*, 268 U.S. 652, at 666).

16 *Malloy*, 378 U.S. 1, at 6.

17 Ibid.

18 Ibid., at 7.

> [t]he Fourteenth Amendment secures against state invasion the same privilege that the Fifth Amendment guarantees against federal infringement—the right of a person to remain silent unless he chooses to speak in the unfettered exercise of his own will, and to suffer no penalty, as held in *Twining*, for such silence.[19]

This overturned the Court's *Twining* refusal to protect self-incrimination from state governments while retaining its Due Process Clause defense of fundamental rights. The *Malloy* majority ruled that due process of law included the fundamental right to be free from compelled self-incrimination.

Brennan elaborated that the prohibition on coerced incriminating statements was so integral to America's justice system that a state may not treat witnesses using "a less stringent standard than is applicable in a federal proceeding."[20] In contrast to the *Palko* defense of rights, Brennan explained that "the constitutional inquiry is not whether the conduct of state officers in obtaining the confession was shocking, but whether the confession was 'free and voluntary.'"[21] He went further, asserting that incorporated rights "are all to be enforced against the States under the Fourteenth Amendment according to the same standards that protect those personal rights against federal encroachment."[22] Consequently, "[t]he Court thus has rejected the notion that the Fourteenth Amendment applies to the States only a 'watered-down, subjective version of the individual guarantees of the Bill of Rights.'"[23]

Confirmation

Justices have often referenced *Malloy* as the decision in which the Court extended the protection against self-incrimination to the states. Justice Arthur Goldberg in *Murphy v. Waterfront Commission* (1964), announced the same day as *Malloy*, began with "[w]e have held today that the Fifth Amendment privilege against self-incrimination must be deemed fully applicable to the States through the Fourteenth Amendment. *Malloy v. Hogan*."[24] Black in *Pointer v. Texas* (1965) described *Malloy* as "holding that the Fifth Amendment's guarantee against self-incrimination was made applicable to the States by the Fourteenth."[25] Returning

19 Ibid., at 8.
20 Ibid., at 10.
21 Ibid., at 7 (citation information omitted; quoting *Bram v. United States*, 168 U.S. 532, at 542 (1897)).
22 *Malloy*, 378 U.S. 1, at 10.
23 Ibid., at 10–11.
24 *Murphy v. Waterfront Commission*, 378 U.S. 52, at 53 (1964).
25 *Pointer v. Texas*, 380 U.S. 400, at 403 (1965) (citation information omitted).

to Goldberg, he confirmed the same in his *Pointer* concurrence.[26] In *Miranda v. Arizona* (1966), Chief Justice Earl Warren stated that "[i]n *Malloy*, we squarely held the privilege applicable to the States, and held that the substantive standards underlying the privilege applied with full force to state court proceedings."[27]

Other justices recognized *Malloy* as the incorporation case in brief notes, such as Justice Byron White in *Duncan v. Louisiana* (1968) listing "the right guaranteed by the Fifth Amendment to be free of compelled self-incrimination" and referencing *Malloy* in the related footnote.[28] Chief Justice William Rehnquist in *Albright v. Oliver* (1994) and Justice Samuel Alito in *McDonald v. Chicago* (2010) made similar confirmations, with Alito simply stating, "*Malloy v. Hogan* (1964) (privilege against self-incrimination)."[29]

Summary

The Court in *Malloy* incorporated the Fifth Amendment right to be free from compulsory self-incrimination. Brennan was clear about this ruling, stating that, like the right to counsel, "the Fifth Amendment's exception from compulsory self-incrimination is also protected by the Fourteenth Amendment against abridgment by the States."[30] He also supplemented the defense of fundamental rights in *Malloy* with the assertion that states must protect incorporated rights by the "same standards" as the federal government. The Court has acknowledged *Malloy* as the case in which it incorporated the federal prohibition against self-incrimination.

26 Ibid., at 412 n. 5 (Goldberg, A., concurring).

27 *Miranda v. Arizona*, 384 U.S. 436, at 467–68 (1966).

28 *Duncan v. Louisiana*, 391 U.S. 145, at 148 n. 7 (1968).

29 *Albright v. Oliver*, 510 U.S. 266, at 273 (1994); and *McDonald v. City of Chicago*, 561 U.S. 742, at 764 n. 12 (2010) (citation information omitted).

30 *Malloy*, 378 U.S. 1, at 6.

Due Process of Law

> "No person shall [...] be deprived of life, liberty, or property, without due process of law."

The Fifth and Fourteenth Amendments share similar due process of law wording, with the exception that the Fifth protects a person from the *federal* government and the Fourteenth protects a person from *state* government ("nor shall any State deprive any person of life, liberty, or property, without due process of law"). The Fifth Amendment presents due process as a distinct right alongside other guarantees. It does not list due process first or otherwise suggest that it encompasses other rights. As Justice Felix Frankfurter explained in his *Malinski v. New York* (1945) concurrence, the Fifth Amendment due process right is not "a shorthand statement of other specific clauses in the same Amendment."[1] The Supreme Court in *Scott v. McNeal* (1894) held that the Fourteenth Amendment protects due process of law against state infringement.[2] Adhering to this view since then, it has not incorporated the Fifth Amendment right of due process.

1 *Malinski v. New York*, 324 U.S. 401, at 415 (1945) (Frankfurter, F., concurring).

2 *Scott v. McNeal*, 154 U.S. 34, at 45 (1894).

Before *Scott*

During the mid-1800s, the Court regarded due process of law as integral to the country's justice system at both national and state levels. The Constitution and Fifth Amendment protected federal due process, whereas states handled their own justice systems. For example, in *Murray's Lessee v. Hoboken Land & Improvement* (1856), Justice Benjamin Curtis argued that states had long followed "due process of law."[3] Referring to due process and the Constitution's Article III protection of federal jury trials, he held that "[w]hen the fifth article of amendment containing the words now in question was made, the trial by jury in criminal cases had thus already been provided for" at the federal level.[4] This was to say that the Fifth Amendment enhanced federal due process of law but did not add anything to the state level.

The addition of the Fourteenth Amendment to the Constitution in 1868 did not alter the Court's view that state and federal governments already followed due process of law, with some justices describing the Due Process Clause as merely a supplementary protection. In *Slaughter-House Cases* (1873), Justice Samuel Miller asserted that the Fifth Amendment ensured due process of law at the federal level while most state constitutions guaranteed due process at the state level.[5] He added, however, that the Fourteenth Amendment "may place the restraining power over the States in this matter in the hands of the Federal government."[6] Without citing *Slaughter-House*, Justice Morrison Waite in *United States v. Cruikshank* (1876) expressed the same perspective, elaborating that

> [t]he Fourteenth Amendment prohibits a State from depriving any person of life, liberty, or property, without due process of law; but this adds nothing to the rights of one citizen as against another. It simply furnishes an additional guaranty against any encroachment by the States upon the fundamental rights which belong to every citizen as a member of society.[7]

Waite struck a similar note in *Walker v. Sauvinet* (1876), explaining that states established their own due process of law requirements, which the Court could evaluate in terms of general due process but not specific Bill of Rights' provisions.[8]

3 *Murray's Lessee v. Hoboken Land & Improvement Co.*, 59 U.S. (18 How.) 272, at 276, 280, 281 (1856).
4 Ibid., at 276.
5 *Slaughter-House Cases*, 83 U.S. (16 Wall.) 36, at 80 (1873).
6 Ibid.
7 *United States v. Cruikshank*, 92 U.S. 542, at 554 (1876).
8 *Walker v. Sauvinet*, 92 U.S. 90, at 92–3 (1876).

In *Davidson v. New Orleans* (1878), Miller argued that due process of law was present at the state level throughout American history.[9] Because the due process of law guarantee of the Fourteenth Amendment was not new, Miller described it as nothing more than a "declaration."[10] The Court could use it to uphold "a fair trial," but not specific judicial procedures.[11]

Justice Stanley Matthews in *Hurtado v. California* (1884) held to this line of reasoning. He elaborated that the Fifth Amendment protected due process against the federal government, whereas the Fourteenth Amendment

> refers to that law of the land in each State, which derives its authority from the inherent and reserved powers of the State, exerted within the limits of those fundamental principles of liberty and justice which lie at the base of all our civil and political institutions.[12]

Matthews added that the people acting through their elected state representatives ultimately determined the specifics of each state's due process procedures. The Court therefore ruled that states did not have to use grand jury hearing indictments in order to satisfy due process. It restated this view of due process in *In re Kemmler* (1890), quoting extensively from *Hurtado*.[13]

Until *Scott*, the Court regarded the Fourteenth Amendment as declaring that states already followed due process of law. Some justices also saw it as permitting the federal government to enforce due process at the state level if necessary. The Court had not used the Due Process Clause to overturn a state law.

However, a federal Circuit Court in *Lavin v. Emigrant Industrial Savings Bank* (S.D. N.Y. 1880) ruled against the state for denying a person the due process of law guarantee of the Fourteenth Amendment. This case was about a state law that allowed the divestment of property based on a court's determination that the owner was deceased and therefore the court did not need to give notice. Federal Judge William Choate held in *Lavin* that the law deprived the owner of due process of law in "direct violation of this constitutional guaranty."[14]

9 *Davidson v. New Orleans*, 96 U.S. 97, at 101–2 (1878).
10 Ibid., at 102.
11 Ibid., at 105.
12 *Hurtado v. People of California*, 110 U.S. 516, at 535 (1884).
13 *In re Kemmler*, 136 U.S. 436, at 448 (1890).
14 *Lavin v. Emigrant Industrial Savings Bank*, 1 F. 641, at 663 (S.D. N.Y. 1880).

Scott v. McNeal (1894)

The *Scott* case addressed the Washington State Supreme Court approval of a government liquidation of a person's property without notification because the county believed that the owner was no longer alive. The state did not regard this as a denial of due process of law. For the Court, however, the Due Process Clause protected individuals from such state violations.

Justice Horace Gray in the 9-0 *Scott* opinion quoted the Due Process and Equal Protection Clauses of the Fourteenth Amendment and held that "[t]hese prohibitions extend to all acts of the state, whether through its legislative, its executive, or its judicial authorities."[15] This was the first Court assertion that the Fourteenth Amendment due process protection of a person's "life, liberty or property" against state encroachment was more than a declaration. Gray elaborated that, among the states, the due process of law guarantee of the Fourteenth Amendment "was intended 'to secure the individual from the arbitrary exercise of the powers of government, unrestrained by the established principles of private rights and distributive justice.'"[16] As such, "[n]o judgment of a court is due process of law, if rendered without jurisdiction in the court, or without notice to the party."[17]

Gray agreed with the lower federal court *Lavin* ruling that for a state to take a person's property without notification is to "deprive him of his property without due process of law, within the meaning of the Fourteenth Amendment."[18] He held that "[t]his court concurs in the proposition, there announced"; namely, if a state government takes a person's property without notification, then it denies "'process of law'" and "'is a direct violation of this constitutional guaranty.'"[19] The Court in *Scott* established that the Due Process Clause of the Fourteenth Amendment protected individuals against state governments.

Confirmation

Since *Scott*, the Court has recognized that the due process protection of the Fourteenth Amendment applies at the state level, negating a reason for

15 *Scott*, 154 U.S. 34, at 45.
16 Ibid. (quoting *Cruikshank*, 92 U.S. 542, at 554).
17 *Scott*, 154 U.S. 34, at 46.
18 Ibid., at 50.
19 Ibid., at 50–51 (citing *Lavin*, 1 F. 641, at 663).

incorporating the same protection of the Fifth Amendment. In the unanimous *Missouri Pacific Railway v. Nebraska* (1896) ruling, Gray reiterated his view, without citing *Scott*, that a state's denial of an aspect of due process of law "is a violation of the Fourteenth Article of the Amendment of the Constitution of the United States."[20] Others have referred to *Scott* as having established this perspective.

In using the Due Process Clause to overturn a state action in *Chicago, Burlington & Quincy Railroad v. Chicago* (1897), Justice John Harlan acknowledged that the Court first used the Fourteenth Amendment due process protection against a state in *Scott*. As he elaborated,

> [t]hese principles were enforced in the recent case of *Scott v. McNeal*, in which it was held that the prohibitions of the Fourteenth Amendment extended to "all acts of the State, whether through its legislative, its executive or its judicial authorities."[21]

Justices have occasionally cited the *Chicago, B & Q* majority as applying the Due Process Clause to the state level, which it did.[22] However, *Chicago, B & Q* was not the first time that the Court had done so, and Harlan in that case recognized *Scott* as having led the way. The Court has since appealed the Due Process Clause of the Fourteenth Amendment many times to protect rights from state governments.

Returning to the Fifth Amendment due process right, the Court regards it as pertaining only to the federal government. It usually expresses this view in contrast with the Fourteenth Amendment guarantee of due process at the state level. For example, Justice Mahlon Pitney in *Coppage v. Kansas* (1915) elaborated that

> if Congress is prevented from arbitrary interference with the liberty of contract because of the "due process" provision of the Fifth Amendment, it is too clear for argument that the states are prevented from the like interference by virtue of the corresponding clause of the Fourteenth Amendment.[23]

Frankfurter in his *Adamson v. California* (1947) concurrence affirmed that "[t]he Due Process Clause of the Fourteenth Amendment has an independent potency, precisely as does the Due Process Clause of the Fifth Amendment in relation to the Federal Government."[24]

20 *Missouri Pacific Railway Co. v. Nebraska*, 164 U.S. 403, at 417 (1896).

21 *Chicago, Burlington & Quincy Railroad Co. v. Chicago*, 166 U.S. 226, at 234 (1897) (citation information omitted; quoting *Scott*, 154 U.S. 34, at 45).

22 See, for example, *Smyth v. Ames*, 169 U.S. 466, at 525–26 (1898); and *Twining v. State of New Jersey*, 211 U.S. 78, at 99–100 (1908).

23 *Coppage v. Kansas*, 236 U.S. 1, at 11 (1915).

24 *Adamson v. California*, 332 U.S. 46, at 66 (1947) (Frankfurter, F., concurring). See also *Mathews v. Eldridge*, 424 U.S. 319, at 332 (1976); and *United States v. Salerno*, 481 U.S. 739, at 746 (1987).

The Court has used the Fifth Amendment due process right to protect people from the federal government, not the states. In some of its freedom of contract cases, such as *Adair v. United States* (1908) and *Adkins v. Children's Hospital* (1923), the Court overturned federal laws as violating the due process guarantee of the Fifth Amendment.[25] It has done the same in decisions regarding non-citizens living in the United States and its territories. In *Wong Wing v. United States* (1896), the Court ruled that the Fifth and Sixth Amendment rights of the accused—including "due process of law"—protected anyone living within the nation's territory from the federal government.[26] The Court has held to this view, with Justice John Paul Stevens in *Mathews v. Diaz* (1976) stating that there are "millions of aliens within the jurisdiction of the United States. The Fifth Amendment, as well as the Fourteenth Amendment, protects every one of these persons from deprivation of life, liberty, or property without due process of law."[27]

The Court has not extended the Fifth Amendment federal due process right to the states. No justice listing of incorporated rights addresses the Fifth Amendment due process protection, including Justice Hugo Black's in *Gideon v. Wainwright* (1963), Justice Byron White's in *Duncan v. Louisiana* (1968), and Justice Samuel Alito's in *McDonald v. Chicago* (2010).[28] All of these are rather comprehensive catalogs of incorporated rights. None mention the Fifth Amendment guarantee.

Summary

For the Court, due process of law is an integral feature of America's justice system, with the Fifth Amendment protecting it against the federal government and—as it ruled in *Scott*—the Fourteenth Amendment guaranteeing it against state infringement. With a focus on the Due Process Clause, Gray stated in *Scott* that the Fourteenth Amendment "prohibitions extend to all acts of the state."[29] The Court confirmed *Scott's* relevance for this view of the Due Process Clause in *Chicago, B & Q*. The Fourteenth Amendment protects due process from state governments; consequently, the Court has not incorporated the due process guarantee of the Fifth Amendment and it remains at the federal level.

25 *Adair v. United States*, 208 U.S. 161, at 176 (1908), and *Adkins v. Children's Hospital of DC*, 261 U.S. 525, at 560–61 (1923).

26 *Wong Wing v. United States*, 163 U.S. 228, at 238 (1896).

27 *Mathews v. Diaz*, 426 U.S. 67, at 77 (1976).

28 *Gideon v. Wainwright*, 372 U.S. 335, at 341–42 n. 4–7 (1963); and *Duncan v. Louisiana*, 391 U.S. 145, at 148–49 n. 4–12 (1968); and *McDonald v. City of Chicago*, 561 U.S. 742, at 764 n. 12 (2010).

29 *Scott*, 154 U.S. 34, at 45.

Just Compensation

"[N]or shall private property be taken for public use, without just compensation"

The first Bill of Rights' guarantee that the Supreme Court extended to the state level was the Fifth Amendment right to just compensation. In *Chicago, Burlington & Quincy Railroad v. Chicago* (1897), it held that the Due Process Clause of the Fourteenth Amendment protected the right of just compensation from state infringement.[1]

Before *Chicago, B & Q*

While the Court in some earlier decisions recognized that states followed due process of law—which included protecting a person's life, liberty, and property—it did not apply the Fifth Amendment right to just compensation to the state level. As government could not take someone's property without following due process of law, the Court intimated that this included just compensation. However, states were expected to work out the details of due process. For example, in *Murray's Lessee v. Hoboken Land & Improvement* (1856), Justice Benjamin Curtis argued

1 *Chicago, Burlington & Quincy Railroad Co. v. Chicago*, 166 U.S. 226, at 234 (1897).

that the nation's basic due process legal system involved protection of a person's property; however, each state controlled its legal procedures.[2]

Justice Samuel Miller in *Davidson v. New Orleans* (1878) agreed that states adhered to due process of law yet retained discretion over the particulars, including just compensation.[3] He pointed to the fact that the Fourteenth Amendment did not mention the right of just compensation.[4] State constitutions and legislatures specified due process guarantees; the Fourteenth Amendment protected only "those principles of general constitutional law," which amounted to "a full and fair hearing."[5] Each state, not the federal government, had authority over "the modes of proceeding applicable to such a case."[6]

The Court in *Chicago, Milwaukee & St. Paul Railway Minnesota* (1890) regarded due process as already existing at the state level and that it included protection of private property. Justice Samuel Blatchford in the majority opinion argued that it was unconstitutional for a state government to deprive a company "of the lawful use of its property, and thus, in substance and effect, of the property itself, without due process of law and in violation of the Constitution of the United States."[7] While Blatchford appealed to familiar principles, he did not reference the Fifth or Fourteenth Amendments. Instead, just compensation, like an investigative hearing, which this case was about, was among the procedural aspects of due process of law.[8] Justice Joseph Bradley agreed with this perspective of due process in his dissent, arguing that "[i]n this matter,—just compensation for property taken for public use,—the states make their own regulations, by constitution, or otherwise."[9]

In *Scott v. McNeal* (1894), a unanimous Court used the Due Process Clause of the Fourteenth Amendment to rule against a state action that took a person's property without first giving notice. While the opinion addressed protection of property, Justice Horace Gray did not mention the Fifth Amendment just compensation right because the case focused on due process of law. However, for the Court, due process necessarily involved several protections, including government notification that it was taking a person's property.[10]

2 *Murray's Lessee v. Hoboken Land & Improvement Co.*, 59 U.S. (18 How.) 272, at 276 (1856).
3 *Davidson v. New Orleans*, 96 U.S. 97, at 101 (1878).
4 Ibid., at 105.
5 Ibid.
6 Ibid.
7 *Chicago, Milwaukee & St. Paul Railway Co. v. Minnesota*, 134 U.S. 418, at 458 (1890).
8 Ibid, at 457.
9 Ibid., at 465 (Bradley, J., dissenting).
10 *Scott v. McNeal*, 154 U.S. 34, at 45–46 (1894).

The Court ruled in *Fallbrook Irrigation District v. Bradley* (1896) that the entire Fifth Amendment, and specifically the just compensation right, only applied to the federal government.[11] Yet, Justice Rufus Peckham argued that while the Fourteenth Amendment did not address just compensation, the Due Process Clause could at least allow the Court to rule on such issues. After all, taking private property for anything other than public use without a hearing or compensating the owner was not due process of law.[12]

Gray in *Missouri Pacific Railway v. Nebraska* (1896) reiterated without citing his *Scott* holding that the due process of law guarantee of the Fourteenth Amendment protected private property at the state level. He concluded that "[t]he taking by a State of the private property of one person or corporation, without the owner's consent, for the private use of another, is not due process of law."[13] This violated the Fourteenth Amendment, Gray asserted; however, rather than just compensation, he was referring to government taking property without the owner's consent.

In these earlier cases, the Court regarded due process of law as deeply ingrained in American civil society and that it included, among other rights, protection against government taking private property without appropriate compensation. Justices have not cited any of these pre-*Chicago, B & Q* cases, however, as incorporating the right of just compensation.

Chicago, Burlington & Quincy Railroad v. Chicago (1897)

The Court applied the Fifth Amendment right of just compensation to the state level in its 7-1 *Chicago, B & Q* holding that the guarantee was an integral part of due process of law. The background of this decision involved a jury awarding a railroad company only $1.00 in compensation for its land that the City of Chicago appropriated to widen a road. Justice John Harlan in *Chicago, B & Q* explored using the Equal Protection Clause since the railroad company argued that Chicago denied both equal protection and due process of law. He held that because the city government had not prevented the company from using its tracks, "there was no denial of the equal protection of the laws," and he focused on the Due Process Clause.[14]

11 *Fallbrook Irrigation District v. Bradley*, 164 U.S. 112, at 158 (1896).
12 Ibid., at 158, 161, 169.
13 *Missouri Pacific Railway Co. v. Nebraska*, 164 U.S. 403, at 417 (1896).
14 *Chicago, B & Q*, 166 U.S. 226, at 258.

Harlan referenced both *Davidson* and *Missouri Pacific* to support the premise that "[d]ue protection of the rights of property has been regarded as a vital principle of republican institutions."[15] The Court already ruled in *Scott*, Harlan explained, that the due process guarantee of the Fourteenth Amendment included protection against states arbitrarily taking private property.[16] He reasoned that, therefore, "due process of law in that amendment is applicable to the direct appropriation by the State to public use and without compensation of the private property of the citizen."[17] Due process protection of a person's property not only required consent and notification, as the Court had previously ruled, but also compensation. Harlan acknowledged that states retained control over the specific procedures of their justice systems; however, these rules must protect the right of just compensation. As he elaborated, "[t]he legislature may prescribe a form of procedure to be observed in the taking of private property for public use, but it is not due process of law if provision be not made for compensation."[18] The right of just compensation was necessary for due process of law and therefore the Due Process Clause included this specific right. Without mentioning the Fifth Amendment directly, he ruled that

> whereby private property is taken for the State or under its direction for public use, without compensation made or secured to the owner, is, upon principle and authority, wanting in the due process of law required by the Fourteenth Amendment.[19]

In other words, the Due Process Clause protected the right of just compensation from state abridgment.

Confirmation

The Court has been unambiguous that it incorporated the Fifth Amendment right to just compensation in *Chicago, B & Q*. Harlan in *Smyth v. Ames* (1898) confirmed that his recent ruling protected the right against states.[20] In his *Adamson v. California* (1947) dissent, Justice Hugo Black explained that the Court held in previous cases that the Fourteenth Amendment guaranteed some "fundamental rights" at the state level, including "the right to receive just compensation

15 Ibid., at 235–36.
16 Ibid., at 234.
17 Ibid., at 236.
18 Ibid., at 236.
19 Ibid., at 241.
20 *Smyth v. Ames*, 169 U.S. 466, at 522, 525–26 (1898).

on account of taking private property for public use, *Chicago, B. & Q. R. Co. v. Chicago*."[21] Several justices providing catalogs of incorporated rights identified *Chicago, B & Q* as the just compensation incorporation case. This includes Black in *Gideon v. Wainwright* (1963), Justice William Brennan in *Malloy v. Hogan* (1964), Justice Arthur Goldberg in *Pointer v. Texas* (1965), Justice Byron White in *Duncan v. Louisiana* (1968), and Justice Samuel Alito in *McDonald v. Chicago* (2010).[22]

Summary

The Court in *Chicago, B & Q* incorporated the Fifth Amendment right of just compensation. For the Court, due process of law necessarily included just compensation. Under the Fourteenth Amendment, Harlan held, "the taking of private property for public use [...] is not due process of law if provision be not made for compensation."[23] The Court has since acknowledged that in *Chicago, B & Q* it extended the Fifth Amendment right of just compensation to the state level.

21 *Adamson v. California*, 332 U.S. 46, at 84–85 (1947) (Black, H., dissenting).

22 *Gideon v. Wainwright*, 372 U.S. 335, at 341–42 n. 5 (1963); *Malloy v. Hogan*, 378 U.S. 1, at 4 (1964); *Pointer v. Texas*, 380 U.S. 400, at 412 n. 4 (1965) (Goldberg, A., concurring); *Duncan v. Louisiana*, 391 U.S. 145, at 148 n. 4 (1968); and *McDonald v. City of Chicago*, 561 U.S. 742, at 764 n. 12 (2010).

23 *Chicago, B & Q*, 166 U.S. 226, at 236.

PART VI

SIXTH AMENDMENT

Speedy Trial

"In all criminal prosecutions, the accused shall enjoy the right to a speedy […] trial."

In *Klopfer v. North Carolina* (1967), the Supreme Court ruled that the Fourteenth Amendment incorporated the Sixth Amendment right to a speedy trial.[1] *Klopfer* was a sharp turn for the Court, as it had long taken a hands-off approach to protecting this federal guarantee at the state level.

Before *Klopfer*

In cases addressing the speedy trial guarantee before *Klopfer*, the Court considered the right at the federal level and regarded it as conditional. Justice Joseph McKenna in *Beavers v. Haubert* (1905) established this perspective, stating that "[w]e do not think the right is so unqualified and absolute. If it is of that character, it determines the order of trial of indictments in the same court."[2] This meant that if the federal government accused a person of more than one crime, then a court could schedule the trials at different times. McKenna elaborated that "[t]he right of a speedy trial

1 *Klopfer v. North Carolina*, 386 U.S. 213 (1967).
2 *Beavers v. Haubert*, 198 U.S. 77, at 86 (1905).

is necessarily relative. It is consistent with delays and depends upon circumstances. It secures rights to a defendant. It does not preclude the rights of public justice."[3]

While the Court continued to rely on the *Beavers* view of the speedy trial protection at the federal level, it began to embrace the importance of the right. For example, Justice Stanley Reed in *Pollard v. United States* (1957), referencing *Beavers*, argued that "[w]hether delay in completing a prosecution such as here occurred amounts to an unconstitutional deprivation of rights depends upon the circumstances. The delay must not be purposeful or oppressive."[4] In *Smith v. United States* (1959), Chief Justice Earl Warren elaborated that "[w]hile justice should be administered with dispatch, the essential ingredient is orderly expedition and not mere speed."[5] After all, he explained, moving too quickly through the indictment process at the federal level could deny the accused due process of law. He added, however, that if "arrest and incarceration are followed by inordinate delay prior to indictment, a defendant may, under appropriate circumstances, invoke the protection of the Sixth Amendment."[6] Justice Byron White in *United States v. Ewell* (1966) echoed this orderly expeditious view, arguing that "[a] requirement of unreasonable speed would have a deleterious effect both upon the rights of the accused and upon the ability of society to protect itself."[7] Regarding speedy trial as an absolute right would disrupt the flexibility necessary for an orderly criminal justice system. The Court would set all these arguments aside, however, when it considered the speedy trial right at the state level in *Klopfer*.

In the years leading up to *Klopfer*, the Court used the Due Process Clause to extend several criminal trial protections to the states. These included the Fifth Amendment right against compulsory self-incrimination in *Malloy v. Hogan* (1964) and Sixth Amendment rights to counsel in *Gideon v. Wainwright* (1963) and confront opposing witnesses in *Pointer v. Texas* (1965).[8]

Klopfer v. North Carolina (1967)

By a 9-0 vote, the Court incorporated the speedy trial right in *Klopfer*. In this case, the Court considered a state law that allowed county prosecutors to stop indictment

3 Ibid., at 87.
4 *Pollard v. United States*, 352 U.S. 354, at 361 (1957) (citation information omitted).
5 *Smith v. United States*, 360 U.S. 1, at 10 (1959).
6 Ibid.
7 *United States v. Ewell*, 383 U.S. 116, at 120 (1966).
8 *Malloy v. Hogan*, 378 U.S. 1 (1964); *Gideon v. Wainwright*, 372 U.S. 335 (1963); and *Pointer v. Texas*, 380 U.S. 400 (1965).

procedures, release the accused, and return to the proceedings at any time. Warren wrote in the opinion that this process "clearly denies the petitioner the right to a speedy trial which we hold is guaranteed to him by the Sixth Amendment of the Constitution of the United States."[9] He did not mention the Court's previous understandings of the right nor reference *Beavers*, *Pollard*, or *Smith*. Warren only noted White's concern from *Ewell* that prolonged prosecution causes the accused to feel "anxiety and concern accompanying public accusation."[10]

For the Court in *Klopfer*, speedy trial was a fundamental right on the same par as other incorporated Sixth Amendment protections. Warren elaborated that the Court in *Gideon* and *Pointer* used the Fourteenth Amendment to apply Sixth Amendment rights to the state level.[11] For example, he agreed with Justice Hugo Black's description in *Pointer* that the Court in several cases held "'various provisions of the Bill of Rights applicable to the States by virtue of the Fourteenth Amendment.'"[12] While Warren did not mention the Due Process Clause, the Court used it in these earlier decisions. He adhered to the *Malloy* standard, which Black also followed in *Pointer*, that states should use federal standards to protect incorporated rights.[13] Warren stated that "[w]e hold here that the right to a speedy trial is as fundamental as any of the rights secured by the Sixth Amendment."[14] He reviewed the history of the speedy trial protection to demonstrate "[t]hat this right was considered fundamental at this early period in our history," and remains "one of the most basic rights preserved by our Constitution."[15]

Confirmation

The Court has often identified *Klopfer* as the decision in which it extended the speedy trial guarantee to the state level. Rare is the instance in which the Court mentions *Klopfer* in relation to incorporation without also including this right. One example is Justice William Douglas in *Argersinger v. Hamlin* (1972), identifying *Klopfer* as a Sixth Amendment incorporation case without specifying the right it protected.[16]

9 *Klopfer*, 386 U.S. 213, at 222.
10 Ibid., at 222 (quoting *Ewell*, 383 U.S. 116, at 120).
11 *Klopfer*, 386 U.S. 213, at 222.
12 Ibid. (quoting *Pointer*, 380 U.S. 400, at 406).
13 *Klopfer*, 386 U.S. 213, at 222–23 (citing *Pointer*, 380 U.S. 400, at 406). See *Malloy*, 378 U.S. 1, at 10.
14 *Klopfer*, 386 U.S. 213, at 223.
15 Ibid., at 225, 226.
16 *Argersinger v. Hamlin*, 407 U.S. 25, at 27 (1972).

Instead, various justices since 1967 have unhesitatingly credited the unanimous *Klopfer* decision as the speedy trial incorporation case. In a listing of incorporated Sixth Amendment rights in *Washington v. Texas* (1967), which the Court announced the same week as *Klopfer*, Warren confirmed that the Court in *Klopfer* held speedy trial applicable to the states.[17] Justice Potter Stewart began *Smith v. Hooey* (1969) with the reminder that "[i]n *Klopfer v. North Carolina*, this Court held that, by virtue of the Fourteenth Amendment, the Sixth Amendment right to a speedy trial is enforceable against the States as 'one of the most basic rights preserved by our Constitution.'"[18] Others acknowledging *Klopfer* as the speedy trial incorporation decision include White in *Duncan v. Louisiana* (1968), Justice William Brennan in his *Dickey v. Florida* (1970) concurrence, Douglas in his *United States v. Marion* (1971) concurrence, Justice Lewis Powell in *Barker v. Wingo* (1972), Chief Justice William Rehnquist in *Albright v. Oliver* (1994), and Justice Samuel Alito in *McDonald v. Chicago* (2010).[19]

Summary

The Court ruled in *Klopfer* that the Sixth Amendment speedy trial right applied at the state level. As Warren concluded, a state may not deny a person accused of a crime "the right to a speedy trial which we hold is guaranteed to him by the Sixth Amendment of the Constitution."[20] Several justices have recognized that the Court incorporated this right in *Klopfer*.

17 *Washington v. Texas*, 388 U.S. 14, at 18 n. 10 (1967).

18 *Smith v. Hooey*, 393 U.S. 374, at 374–75 (1969) (citation information omitted; citing *Klopfer*, 386 U.S. 213, at 226).

19 *Duncan v. Louisiana*, 391 U.S. 145, at 148 n. 9 (1968); *Dickey v. Florida*, 398 U.S. 30, at 39–40, 50 (1970) (Brennan, W., concurring); *United States v. Marion*, 404 U.S. 307, at 330 (1971) (Douglas, W., concurring); *Barker v. Wingo*, 407 U.S. 514, at 515 (1972); *Albright v. Oliver*, 510 U.S. 266, at 273 (1994); and *McDonald v. City of Chicago*, 561 U.S. 742, at 764 n. 12 (2010).

20 *Klopfer*, 386 U.S. 213, at 222.

Public Trial

"In all criminal prosecutions, the accused shall enjoy the right to a [...] public trial."

In the case of *In re Oliver* (1948), the Supreme Court held that the Due Process Clause of the Fourteenth Amendment included the Sixth Amendment right to a public trial, thereby preventing states from denying it to the accused.[1] This is also known as the right "to be heard" in criminal prosecutions.[2]

Before *Oliver*

The Court suggested previously to *Oliver* that the due process protection of the Fourteenth Amendment could include the public trial right. In *Gaines v. Washington* (1928), the Court did not accept the claim that a state trial judge's announcement forbidding public observation of court proceedings denied the federal public trial right.[3] To begin with, Chief Justice William Taft explained that, like all amendments

1 *In re Oliver*, 333 U.S. 257 (1948).

2 See, for example, *Holden v. Hardy*, 169 U.S. 366, at 390 (1898); *Powell v. Alabama*, 287 U.S. 45, at 68 (1932); *Snyder v. Massachusetts*, 291 U.S. 97, at 116 (1943); and *Oliver*, 333 U.S. 257, at 273, 275, 278.

3 *Gaines v. Washington*, 277 U.S. 81, at 84–5 (1928).

of the Bill of Rights, "the Sixth Amendment to the Federal Constitution does not apply to the trial of criminal prosecutions by a State."[4] For support, he referenced *Spies v. Illinois* (1887), which in turn cited *Barron v. Baltimore* (1833) and cases affirming the *Barron* view that the Bill of Rights only pertained to the federal government.[5] Taft then intimated that the Due Process Clause could protect against secret state trials; however, "[t]he question has not arisen in any case cited to us."[6] Moreover, "even if the due process clause requires the same kind of public trial as that contended for by the petitioner, the record does not disclose facts which would justify us in bringing the case before us for our review."[7]

Before *Oliver*, the Court had extended some federal rights to the state level; namely, religious establishment, religious exercise, speech, press, assembly, reasonable searches and seizures, just compensation, and counsel for capital crimes. For most of these rulings, the Court reasoned that the Due Process Clause protected such fundamental rights. Justice Benjamin Cardozo in *Palko v. Connecticut* (1937) developed a competing rationale, which considered violations case-by-case, only ruling them unconstitutional if they were so "shocking" as to threaten a fundamental principle of "ordered liberty."[8]

In re Oliver (1948)

The Court in *Oliver* held that the Sixth Amendment right to a public trial existed at all levels of government in the United States. At issue was Michigan's "one-man grand jury" investigation law that allowed judges to conduct indictment hearings behind closed doors. In this case, the judge apparently heard from a witness without the defendant present and then pronounced the sentence.

Justice Hugo Black in the majority 7-2 opinion argued that the nation's traditions and practices of due process of law included the public trial right. He asserted that no secret criminal trial had ever occurred in the United States because the nation has a "universal rule against secret trials."[9] Black explained that in the earlier case of *Gaines*, "this Court assumed that a criminal trial conducted in

4 Ibid., at 85.

5 Ibid. (citing *Spies v. Illinois*, 123 U.S. 131, at 166 (1887)). See *Barron ex rel. Tiernan v. City of Baltimore*, 32 U.S. (7 Pet.) 243, at 247 (1833).

6 *Gaines*, 277 U.S. 81, at 85.

7 Ibid., at 86.

8 *Palko v. Connecticut*, 302 U.S. 319, at 325, 328 (1937).

9 *Oliver*, 333 U.S. 257, at 266.

secret would violate the procedural requirements of the Fourteenth Amendment's due process clause."[10] Now, in *Oliver*, Black ruled that

> [i]n view of this nation's historic distrust of secret proceedings, their inherent dangers to freedom, and the universal requirement of our federal and state governments that criminal trials be public, the Fourteenth Amendment's guarantee that no one shall be deprived of his liberty without due process of law means at least that an accused cannot be thus sentenced to prison.[11]

The Due Process Clause protection of liberty included the right to public criminal trials.

For Black, the public trial guarantee was a fundamental aspect of due process of law. As he elaborated, "[a] person's right to reasonable notice of a charge against him, and an opportunity to be heard in his defense—a right to his day in court—are basic in our system of jurisprudence."[12] Among the cases he referenced in support of this defense of basic rights were *Snyder v. Massachusetts* (1934), *Powell v. Alabama* (1932), and *Holden v. Hardy* (1898).[13] On the pages he cited in these decisions, the Court argued that some due process rights—including "an opportunity to be heard"—are "obviously fundamental" and "indispensable" (*Snyder*), "fundamental" and "constitute basic elements of the constitutional requirement of due process of law" (*Powell*), and "natural and inherent principles of justice" (*Holden*).

Black emphasized that there would be no due process of law in the United States without public trials. He summarized that

> [t]he right to be heard in open court before one is condemned is too valuable to be whittled away under the guise of "demoralization of the court's authority." It is "the law of the land" that no man's life, liberty or property be forfeited as a punishment until there has been a charge fairly made and fairly tried in a public tribunal.[14]

Public trial was among several necessary rights of due process of law at both federal and state levels of government.

10 Ibid., at 272 (citing *Gaines*, 277 U.S. 81, at 85).

11 *Oliver*, 333 U.S. 257, at 273.

12 Ibid.

13 Ibid., at 273 n. 31 (citing, along with other cases, *Snyder*, 291 U.S. 97, at 116; *Powell*, 287 U.S. 45, at 68; and *Holden*, 169 U.S. 366, at 390).

14 *Oliver*, 333 U.S. 257, at 278 (quoting from *Cooke v. United States*, 267 U.S. 517, at 536 (1928); and *Chambers v. Florida*, 309 U.S. 227, at 236 (1940)).

Confirmation

Several justices have confirmed that the Court in *Oliver* applied the right to a public jury trial to the states. A few have cited this decision as protecting only "jury trial," leaving aside "public trial."[15] Several others, however, have clearly regarded *Oliver* as the decision in which the Court extended the federal public trial guarantee to the state level.

In another decision that he authored, *In re Murchison* (1955), Black affirmed that a state criminal justice system "cannot, consistently with the Due Process Clause of the Fourteenth Amendment, summarily convict a witness of contempt for conduct in the secret hearings. *In re Oliver*."[16] Other justices have recognized that the Court in *Oliver* applied the public trial right to the states. For example, Chief Justice Earl Warren in explaining the Court's recent protection of federal criminal justice rights in *Estes v. Texas* (1965) stated "that the fundamental conception of a fair trial includes many of the specific provisions of the Sixth Amendment, such as the right to have the proceedings open to the public, *In re Oliver*."[17] He also credited *Oliver* as the incorporation case for the public trial right in *Washington v. Texas* (1967).[18] Several more justices have similarly explained that the Court protected public trials against state infringement in *Oliver*. These include Justice Byron White in *Duncan v. Louisiana* (1968), Justice William Douglas in *Argersinger v. Hamlin* (1972), Justice Potter Stewart in *Gannett v. DePasquale* (1979), and Justice Harry Blackmun in his partially concurring opinion of that decision.[19] Justice Samuel Alito in *McDonald v. Chicago* (2010) described that "[t]he Court eventually incorporated almost all of the provisions of the Bill of Rights," among which he included "*In re Oliver* (right to a public trial)."[20]

15 See *Irvin v. Dowd*, 366 U.S. 717, at 722 (1961); and *Turner v. Louisiana*, 379 U.S. 466, at 471 (1965); see also the brief mention in *Faretta v. California*, 422 U.S. 806, at 818 n. 14 (1975).

16 *In re Murchison*, 349 U.S. 133, at 134 (1955).

17 *Estes v. Texas*, 381 U.S. 532, at 560 (1965) (Warren, E. concurring).

18 *Washington v. Texas*, 388 U.S. 14, at 18 n. 11 (1967).

19 *Duncan v. Louisiana*, 391 U.S. 145, at 148 n. 10 (1968); *Argersinger v. Hamlin*, 407 U.S. 25, at 27–28 (1972); and *Gannett Co. v. DePasquale*, 443 U.S. 368, at 380; 414 (Blackmun, H., partial dissenting) (1979).

20 *McDonald v. City of Chicago*, 561 U.S. 742, at 764 n. 12 (2010) (citation information omitted).

Summary

The Court in *Oliver* ruled that a person accused of a crime at the state level has the right to a public trial. The Due Process Clause, Black held, encompassed "the universal requirement of our federal and state governments that criminal trials be public."[21] Many justices have agreed that the Court in *Oliver* extended the public trial right to the states.

21 *Oliver*, 333 U.S. 257, at 273.

Impartial Jury

> "In all criminal prosecutions, the accused shall enjoy the right to a [...] trial, by an impartial jury."

Among Sixth Amendment criminal jury trial rights is "an impartial jury." As with some other Bill of Rights' trial protections, justices regarded impartial jury as a feature of due process of law before protecting it against states. The Supreme Court incorporated this right into the Due Process Clause in *Parker v. Gladden* (1966).[1]

Before *Parker*

The Court often addressed the importance of impartiality in the criminal justice system before 1966. For example, Justice Oliver Wendell Holmes in *Patterson v. Colorado* (1907) asserted that "[t]he theory of our system is that the conclusions to be reached in a case will be induced only by evidence and argument in open court, and not by any outside influence, whether of private talk or public print."[2] The Court ruled in *Tumey v. Ohio* (1927) that the Fourteenth Amendment

1 *Parker v. Gladden*, 385 U.S. 363 (1966).

2 *Patterson v. Colorado*, 205 U.S. 454, at 462 (1907).

protected defendants against biased judges at the state level but did not mention the Sixth Amendment or any specific right, including impartial jury.[3]

Following the same general due process of law argument, Justice Tom Clark in *Irvin v. Dowd* (1961) explained that "[a]lthough this Court has said that the Fourteenth Amendment does not demand the use of jury trials in a State's criminal procedure, every State has constitutionally provided trial by jury."[4] "In essence," he continued, "the right to jury trial guarantees to the criminally accused a fair trial by a panel of impartial, 'indifferent' jurors. The failure to accord an accused a fair hearing violates even the minimal standards of due process."[5] Clark added that it would be unreasonable to expect jurors not to have heard about a case or hold opinions about guilt or innocence.[6] While Clark in *Irvin* explained that the right of an impartial jury was an essential feature of basic due process of law, he did not appeal to the Sixth or Fourteenth Amendments or argue that the federal right pressed upon the states. A couple of justices have referenced the case as extending the right to the state level, but *Irvin* does not provide an incorporation statement.[7]

The Court provided another example of what violated the concepts of impartial jurors and a fair trial in *Turner v. Louisiana* (1965).[8] In this decision, authored by Justice Potter Stewart, the Court ruled that jury custodial officers who testified for the prosecution in a state-level trial denied the accused a fair and impartial jury.[9] Stewart relied on the *Irvin* definition of a jury as one that is impartial and did not reference the Sixth Amendment or impartial jury right.[10]

The Court specifically mentioned the right of impartial jury in *Singer v. United States* (1965). It ruled against whether the defendant could exercise the opposite of Sixth Amendment rights without court approval, such as having a judge-only instead of a jury trial. The exception, Chief Justice Earl Warren elaborated, was "an impartial trial by jury."[11] With a court's consent, a defendant could waive the right to a jury trial; however, if there was a jury, then it had to be impartial. Warren presented this as an example and did not hold that the federal impartial jury right limited state governments.

3 *Tumey v. Ohio*, 273 U.S. 510, at 523, see also 535 (1927).
4 *Irvin v. Dowd*, 366 U.S. 717, at 721 (1961) (citation information omitted).
5 Ibid., at 722.
6 Ibid., at 723.
7 *Duncan v. Louisiana*, 391 U.S. 145, at 179 n. 17, 182 n. 19 (1968) (Harlan, J., dissenting); and *Groppi v. Wisconsin*, 400 U.S. 505, at 515 (1971) (Black, H., dissenting).
8 *Turner v. Louisiana*, 379 U.S. 466 (1965).
9 Ibid., at 467–68, 471.
10 Ibid., at 471–72.
11 *Singer v. United States*, 380 U.S. 24, at 36 (1965).

In *Sheppard v. Maxwell* (1966), a case that concerned tremendous media publicity, Clark argued that the Court followed the "undeviating rule" of fairness and quoted the passage from *Patterson* that only evidence and courtroom arguments should determine verdicts.[12] Moreover, he asserted that "[d]ue process requires that the accused receive a trial by an impartial jury free from outside influences."[13] The Court in *Sheppard*, however, did not extend the impartial jury right to the state level, instead holding that courts must prevent "prejudicial outside interferences."[14]

Parker v. Gladden (1966)

Unlike the earlier decisions that touched on impartiality, the Court incorporated the right to an impartial jury in *Parker*, a short unsigned 8-1 opinion. This case concerned whether a bailiff commenting that the defendant was guilty biased any of the jurors. The Court stated at the front of the opinion that

> [w]e believe that the statements of the bailiff to the jurors are controlled by the command of the Sixth Amendment, made applicable to the States through the Due Process Clause of the Fourteenth Amendment. It guarantees that "the accused shall enjoy the right to a … trial, by an impartial jury … [and] be confronted with the witnesses against him."[15]

This was the first case in which the Court made such a direct statement as to the incorporation status of the impartial jury right.

The opinion defended impartial juries as necessary for due process of law in relation to confrontation. The bailiff's "expressions were 'private talk,' tending to reach the jury by 'outside influence'"; however, "he was not subjected to confrontation, cross-examination or other safeguards guaranteed to the petitioner."[16] In other words, if the bailiff had been a witness providing evidence against the accused, then the defendant would have had the opportunity to confront and cross-examine him. While the bailiff did not make his comments on the witness stand, at least three jurors heard his prejudicial views. The *Parker* opinion elaborated that "the official character of the bailiff—as an officer of the court as well as the

12 *Sheppard v. Maxwell*, 384 U.S. 333, at 351 (1966).
13 Ibid., at 362.
14 Ibid., at 363.
15 *Parker*, 385 U.S. 363, at 364 (ellipses and interpolation in original; quoting U.S. Bill of Rights, Sixth Amendment).
16 *Parker*, 385 U.S. 363, at 364 (quoting *Patterson*, 205 U.S. 454, at 462).

State—beyond question carries great weight with a jury."[17] One juror testified that the bailiff's comments swayed her to find the defendant guilty.

The Court ruled that "we believe that the unauthorized conduct of the bailiff 'involves such a probability that prejudice will result that it is deemed inherently lacking in due process.'"[18] Due process of law requires the absence of prejudice. The majority opinion referenced *Turner* to emphasize the Court's views that the Constitution protects defendants' basic judicial rights and that a bailiff's expressed opinions could sway jurors.[19] It made no mention of *Tumey* or *Irvin*. The actual number of biased jurors did not matter because the "petitioner was entitled to be tried by 12, not 9 or even 10, impartial and unprejudiced jurors."[20] Justice John Harlan II in his dissent cited *Irvin* but only to support that he knew "of no case in which this Court has held that jurors must have been absolutely insulated from all expressions of opinion on the merits of the case or the judicial process."[21]

Confirmation

The Court has since stated that the federal impartial jury guarantee extends to the state level but not clearly recognized *Parker* as the case in which it incorporated this right. None of the post-1966 justice listings of incorporated rights, including Justice Samuel Alito's, identify *Parker*, let alone any case, as protecting impartial jury from state violation.[22] Several reasons may account for why justices have not credited *Parker* for this development. To begin with, the *Parker* opinion described impartial jury in reference to confronting opposing witnesses. *Parker* may also not receive much attention because the Court had not yet incorporated the jury trial right into the Due Process Clause in 1966. Additionally, some justices have used a different concept when addressing impartial juries.

Justices have tended to focus on "fair cross section" as a way for states to ensure impartial juries, a concept the Court did not use in *Parker*. For example, Justice Byron White in *Taylor v. Louisiana* (1975) held that "the Louisiana jury selection system deprived appellant of his Sixth and Fourteenth Amendment right to an impartial jury trial" because it did not draw the jury of the case "from a venire

17 *Parker*, 385 U.S. 363, at 365.

18 Ibid. (citation information omitted; quoting *Estes v. Texas*, 381 U.S. 532, at 542–43 (1965)).

19 *Parker*, 385 U.S. 363, at 365.

20 Ibid., at 366.

21 Ibid., at 367 (Harlan, J., dissenting).

22 *Washington v. Texas*, 388 U.S. 14, at 18 (1967); *Duncan*, 391 U.S. 145, at 148; and *McDonald v. City of Chicago*, 561 U.S. 742, at 764 n. 12 (2010).

constituting a fair cross section of the community."[23] Justice Antonin Scalia in *Holland v. Illinois* (1990) regarded the Sixth Amendment as protecting the fair cross section requirement. Quoting the Sixth Amendment passage containing "by an impartial jury," he admitted that "[t]he fair-cross-section venire requirement is obviously not explicit in this text, but is derived from the traditional understanding of how an 'impartial jury' is assembled."[24] Scalia emphasized that "[t]he Sixth Amendment requirement of a fair cross section on the venire is a means of assuring, not a *representative* jury (which the Constitution does not demand), but an *impartial* one (which it does)."[25]

While the justices did not rely on *Parker* in these cases, they referred to the impartial jury trial right as existing at the state level. Harlan in his *Duncan v. Louisiana* (1968) dissent and Justice William Brennan in his *Dickey v. Florida* (1970) concurrence included impartial jury along with other incorporated Sixth Amendment rights but did not reference *Parker*.[26] Justice William Rehnquist in his *Duren v. Missouri* (1979) dissent criticized the Court's appeal to fair cross section and stated plainly that "[t]he Sixth and Fourteenth Amendments guarantee a criminal defendant the right to be tried by an impartial jury."[27]

Another possible reason for the Court's neglect of *Parker* as the impartial jury incorporation case is because due process of law requires impartiality from the entire justice system, not just from juries. As Brennan explained in his *Dickey* concurrence, regarding Sixth Amendment "safeguards, prejudice is usually assumed when any of them is shown to have been denied."[28] In his *Duncan* dissent, Harlan elaborated that the Court "by interpretation of the phrase 'due process of law,' enforced the Constitution's guarantee that no State may imprison an individual except by fair and impartial procedures."[29] While the Court regards impartial jury as protected at all levels of government, it also views state obstruction of any criminal justice right, such as public trial or legal counsel, as interfering with impartiality. The Court may not find it necessary to focus attention only on impartial jury.

A lower federal court, however, confirmed that the Court in *Parker* extended the impartial jury right to the state level. Judge Sterry Waterman in *United States v. McMann* (2d Cir. 1967) plainly stated that

23 *Taylor v. Louisiana*, 419 U.S. 522, at 525, 526 (1975).
24 *Holland v. Illinois*, 493 U.S. 474, at 480 (1990).
25 Ibid. (emphasis in original).
26 *Duncan*, 391 U.S. 145, at 179 (Harlan, J., dissenting); and *Dickey v. Florida*, 398 U.S. 30, at 54 (1970) (Brennan, W., concurring).
27 *Duren v. Missouri*, 439 U.S. 357, at 378 (1979) (Rehnquist, W., dissenting).
28 *Dickey*, 398 U.S. 30, at 54–55 (Brennan, W., concurring).
29 *Duncan*, 391 U.S. 145, at 177 (Harlan, J., dissenting).

> [i]n *Parker v. Gladden*, the United States Supreme Court has unequivocally held that the right of a defendant in a state criminal prosecution to the full judicial protection of a trial by an impartial jury and the confrontation of the witnesses against him includes the right to protection from outside influences exerted upon the jurors.[30]

The Court has not provided such a clear acknowledgment that in *Parker* it protected the impartial jury guarantee from state governments. It has come close, though. Justice Thurgood Marshall in *Tanner v. United States* (1987) stated that if "[i]f only one juror were shown to be incompetent, the verdict could not stand. Cf. *Parker v. Gladden*."[31] In *United States v. Olano* (1993), Justice Sandra Day O'Connor cited *Parker* as one of a few cases in which the Court had "analyzed outside intrusions upon the jury for prejudicial impact."[32]

Summary

The Court incorporated the impartial jury trial right in *Parker*. The opinion held that the bailiff's biased commentary to jury members was unconstitutional because "of the Sixth Amendment, made applicable to the States through the Due Process Clause of the Fourteenth Amendment. It guarantees that 'the accused shall enjoy the right to a … trial, by an impartial jury.'"[33] While the Court also addressed the confrontation clause, it held that due process required impartial jurors. Justices have confirmed that the right of impartial jury applies at the state level; however, they have not clearly credited *Parker* as the incorporation case.

30 *United States ex rel. DeLucia v. McMann*, 373 F.2d 759, at 762 (2d Cir. 1967) (citation information omitted).

31 *Tanner v. United States*, 483 U.S. 107, at 136–37 n. 4, see also 137 (1987) (Marshall, T., dissenting).

32 *United States v. Olano*, 507 U.S. 725, at 738 (1993).

33 *Parker*, 385 U.S. 363, at 364 (ellipses in original; quoting U.S. Bill of Rights, Sixth Amendment).

Jury Trial

> "In all criminal prosecutions, the accused shall enjoy the right to a [...] trial, by [...] jury."

While the Sixth Amendment is clearly about jury trials for people accused of crimes, the trial by jury right itself is drawn from the longer passage of "the right to a speedy and public trial, by an impartial jury." One of the few rights that the body of the U.S. Constitution protects is "jury trial" for federal criminal cases.[1] The Supreme Court has long presumed that state constitutions protected jury trials at the state level. In *Duncan v. Louisiana* (1968), however, it incorporated the Bill of Rights' guarantee of a jury trial into the Due Process Clause.[2]

Before *Duncan*

For years, the Court held that the Sixth Amendment jury trial right did not extend to the state level because these governments already used due process of law, which included jury trials. Justice Benjamin Curtis made this argument in *Murray's Lessee*

1 U.S. Constitution, Article III, Section 2.
2 *Duncan v. Louisiana*, 391 U.S. 145 (1968).

v. Hoboken Land & Improvement (1856), elaborating that the Bill of Rights simply added more detail to the U.S. Constitution's Article III federal jury trial right.[3] The Court in *Hurtado v. California* (1884) regarded state and federal governments as having their own due process jury trial protections.[4]

In *Maxwell v. Dow* (1900), the Court held against protecting the Sixth Amendment jury trial right against states, with Justice Rufus Peckham asserting that Bill of Rights' guarantees "were intended as restraints and limitations upon the powers of the General Government, and were not intended to, and did not, have any effect upon the powers of the respective States."[5] Making extensive reference to *Slaughter-House Cases* (1873), he insisted that states had their own civil liberty protections.[6] Pointing to *Hurtado* and *Maxwell* for precedent, Justice Horace Lurton in *Jordan v. Massachusetts* (1912) flatly asserted that the Fourteenth Amendment "requirement of due process does not deprive a state of the power to dispense with jury trial altogether."[7]

The Court held a similar view of the federal jury trial right in some later cases. In discussing the Fourteenth Amendment in *Snyder v. Massachusetts* (1934), Justice Benjamin Cardozo argued that a state "is free to regulate the procedure of its courts in accordance with its own conception of policy and fairness, unless in so doing it offends some principle of justice so rooted in the traditions and conscience of our people as to be ranked as fundamental."[8] Just because the Court thought a state criminal justice procedure was unfair or inadequate did not necessarily mean it violated the Fourteenth Amendment. For Cardozo, "[c]onsistently with that amendment, trial by jury may be abolished."[9] He expressed the same perspective in *Palko v. Connecticut* (1937) regarding the Sixth and Seventh Amendments, stating that "[t]his court has ruled that consistently with those amendments trial by jury may be modified by a state or abolished altogether."[10] Along with some other trial rights, he asserted that jury trial was not fundamental to the nation's "scheme of ordered liberty" and therefore state denial of it was not "acute and shocking."[11] Referencing *Palko*, Justice Robert Jackson in *Fay v. New York* (1947) explained that "the commandments of the Sixth and Seventh Amendments, which require jury

3 *Murray's Lessee v. Hoboken Land & Improvement Co.*, 59 U.S. (18 How.) 272, at 276–77 (1856).
4 *Hurtado v. People of California*, 110 U.S. 516, at 532–34 (1884).
5 *Maxwell v. Dow*, 176 U.S. 581, at 586 (1900).
6 Ibid., at 587–92 (citing *Slaughter-House Cases*, 83 U.S. (16 Wall.) 36 (1873)).
7 *Jordan v. Massachusetts*, 225 U.S. 167, at 176 (1912).
8 *Snyder v. Massachusetts*, 291 U.S. 97, at 105 (1934).
9 Ibid.
10 *Palko v. Connecticut*, 302 U.S. 319, at 324 (1937) (citing *Maxwell*, 176 U.S. 581 and other cases).
11 *Palko*, 302 U.S. 319, at 325, 328.

trial in criminal and certain civil cases, are not picked up by the due process clause of the Fourteenth so as to become limitations on the states."[12]

The Court gave some support to the jury trial right at the state level in *Irvin v. Dowd* (1961). Justice Tom Clark explained that, while it was not a Fourteenth Amendment requirement, state constitutions already provided for jury trials.[13] At a minimum, as the Court ruled in earlier cases including *In re Oliver* (1948), he elaborated that state jury trials must be fair and impartial to satisfy the country's due process of law expectations.[14]

During the 1960s, the Court applied several federal criminal trial rights to the states. These incorporated rights included the Fifth Amendment right against compulsory self-incrimination and Sixth Amendment rights to counsel for serious charges, confront opposing witnesses, impartial jury trials, compulsory process for obtaining favorable witnesses, and speedy trials.[15] With some variation, the Court appealed to the Due Process Clause protection of fundamental rights in these decisions. In *Duncan*, it would clarify this incorporation defense.

Duncan v. Louisiana (1968)

The Court incorporated the criminal jury trial right in *Duncan*. This case concerned what many states regarded as petty crimes that did not require a jury trial yet could result in rather harsh sentences, such as two years in prison. The Court ruled 7-2 that the Sixth Amendment jury trial protection covered misdemeanors when defendants faced such significant punishments.

Justice Byron White, authoring the *Duncan* opinion, held that jury trial was a "fundamental right" of the nation's "scheme of justice" and therefore the Due Process Clause of the Fourteenth Amendment protected it at the state level.[16] He identified Bill of Rights' guarantees that the Court already extended to the states using the Due Process Clause, from just compensation to favorable witness, along with their respective cases.[17] Some of these decisions appealed to the idea of

12 *Fay v. New York,* 332 U.S. 261, at 288 (1947).

13 *Irvin v. Dowd,* 366 U.S. 717, at 721–22 (1961).

14 Ibid., at 722 (citing *In re Oliver,* 333 U.S. 257 (1948); *Tumey v. Ohio,* 273 U.S. 510 (1927); and *In re Murchison,* 349 U.S. 133, at 136 (1955)).

15 *Malloy v. Hogan,* 378 U.S. 1 (1964) (no self-incrimination); *Gideon v. Wainwright,* 372 U.S. 335 (1963) (counsel); *Pointer v. Texas,* 380 U.S. 400 (1965) (confrontation); *Parker v. Gladden,* 385 U.S. 363 (1966) (impartial jury); *Washington v. Texas,* 388 U.S. 14 (1967) (defense witness); and *Klopfer v. North Carolina,* 386 U.S. 213 (1967) (speedy trial).

16 *Duncan,* 391 U.S. 145, at 149, see also 154, 150, 157–58.

17 Ibid., at 148 n. 4–12.

fundamental rights. White elaborated that the Court in *Powell v. Alabama* (1932) borrowed from *Hebert v. Louisiana* (1926) to ask if the right of counsel for capital offenses was among "'fundamental principles of liberty and justice which lie at the base of all our civil and political institutions.'"[18] The question posed in *Oliver* was whether the right of public trial was "basic in our system of jurisprudence."[19] In *Gideon v. Wainwright* (1963), *Malloy v. Hogan* (1964), and *Pointer v. Texas* (1965), he explained, the justices determined if the respective Bill of Rights' protection was "a fundamental right, essential to a fair trial," which was a phrase from *Betts v. Brady* (1942).[20] White presented a rephrased rationale that brought these various "tests" together.

Summarizing the defense for incorporating the Sixth Amendment jury trial right, White ruled that

> [b]ecause we believe that trial by jury in criminal cases is fundamental to the American scheme of justice, we hold that the Fourteenth Amendment guarantees a right of jury trial in all criminal cases which—were they to be tried in a federal court—would come within the Sixth Amendment's guarantee.[21]

This "fundamental to the American scheme of justice" defense dropped Cardozo's concepts of "rooted in the traditions" and "acute and shocking," while retaining his *Palko* "scheme of ordered liberty." In a note, for example, White elaborated that the Court was asking if "a particular procedure is fundamental—whether, that is, a procedure is necessary to an Anglo-American regime of ordered liberty."[22] Putting it slightly differently, he explained that the Court recently incorporated several trial rights by determining that each one was "fundamental in the context of the criminal processes maintained by the American States."[23] The Court rejected the *Snyder* and *Palko* "dicta asserting that the right to jury trial is not essential to ordered liberty and may be dispensed with by the States regardless of the Sixth and Fourteenth Amendments."[24]

Unlike the *Snyder-Palko* incorporation approach, White's "American scheme of justice" rested on the very reason for rights. He explained that jury trials were

18 Ibid., at 148 (quoting *Powell v. Alabama*, 287 U.S. 45, at 67 (1932)). See *Hebert v. Louisiana*, 272 U.S. 312, at 316 (1926).

19 *Duncan*, 391 U.S. 145, at 149 (quoting *Oliver*, 333 U.S. 257, at 273).

20 *Duncan*, 391 U.S. 145, at 149 (quoting *Gideon*, 372 U.S. 335, at 343–44; *Malloy*, 378 U.S. 1, at 6; and *Pointer*, 380 U.S. 400, at 403). See *Betts v. Brady*, 316 U.S. 455, at 465 (1942).

21 *Duncan*, 391 U.S. 145, at 149.

22 Ibid., at 149–50 n. 14.

23 Ibid.

24 Ibid., at 155.

fundamental in the American justice system because they prevented the abuse of government power. As White described it, jury trial is "an inestimable safeguard against the corrupt or overzealous prosecutor and against the compliant, biased, or eccentric judge."[25] Stemming from the time of the U.S. founding, he continued, "the jury trial provisions in the Federal and State Constitutions reflect a fundamental decision about the exercise of official power—a reluctance to entrust plenary powers over the life and liberty of the citizen to one judge or to a group of judges."[26] These constitutional guarantees display a "deep commitment of the Nation to the right of jury trial in serious criminal cases as a defense against arbitrary law enforcement" and, White reasoned, this "qualifies for protection under the Due Process Clause of the Fourteenth Amendment, and must therefore be respected by the States."[27]

White asserted more than once that the Court was extending the Sixth Amendment criminal jury trial protection to the states. For example, he explained that the Court's holding was "that the right to jury trial in serious criminal cases is a fundamental right and hence must be recognized by the States as part of their obligation to extend due process of law to all persons within their jurisdiction."[28]

Confirmation

Justices have often recognized that the Court in *Duncan* incorporated the Sixth Amendment criminal jury trial right. For example, Justice Thurgood Marshall in *Benton v. Maryland* (1969), explained that

> [o]nly last Term we found that the right to trial by jury in criminal cases was "fundamental to the American scheme of justice," *Duncan v. Louisiana* (1968), and held that the Sixth Amendment right to a jury trial was applicable to the States through the Fourteenth Amendment.[29]

Other acknowledgments that the Court in *Duncan* applied the federal the criminal jury trial guarantee to the state level include White in *Baldwin v. New York* (1970), Justice William Douglas in *Argersinger v. Hamlin* (1972), Justice Harry Blackmun in his *Gannett v. DePasquale* (1979) dissent, Chief Justice William Rehnquist in his short list of incorporated trial rights in *Albright v. Oliver* (1994), Justice Sandra

25 Ibid., at 156.
26 Ibid.
27 Ibid.
28 Ibid., at 154, see also 157–58.
29 *Benton v. Maryland*, 395 U.S. 784, at 794 (1969) (citation information omitted).

Day O'Connor in *Lewis v. United States* (1996), Justice Anthony Kennedy in his *Lewis* concurrence, and Justice Samuel Alito in his listing of incorporated rights in *McDonald v. Chicago* (2010).[30] As recently as *Ramos v. Louisiana* (2020), Justice Brett Kavanaugh stated that "the Fourteenth Amendment incorporates the Sixth Amendment jury trial right against the States. See *Duncan v. Louisiana* (1968)."[31]

Summary

The *Duncan* majority extended the Sixth Amendment criminal jury trial right to the states. As White explained, "in the American States, as in the federal judicial system, a general grant of jury trial for serious offenses is a fundamental right."[32] The Court has confirmed several times that it incorporated this right in *Duncan*.

30 *Baldwin v. New York* 399 U.S. 66, at 68 (1970); *Argersinger v. Hamlin*, 407 U.S. 25, at 29 (1972); *Gannett Co. v. DePasquale*, 443 U.S. 368, at 415–16 (1979); *Albright v. Oliver*, 510 U.S. 266, at 273 (1994); *Lewis v. United States*, 518 U.S. 322, at 325; 331 (Kennedy, A., concurring) (1996); and *McDonald v. City of Chicago*, 561 U.S. 742, at 764 n. 12 (2010).

31 *Ramos v. Louisiana*, 590 U.S. ___, at 10–11 (2020) (Kavanaugh, B., concurring).

32 *Duncan*, 391 U.S. 145, at 157–58.

Jury of Same State and District as Crime

> "In all criminal prosecutions, the accused shall enjoy the right to a [...] trial, by [...] jury of the State and district wherein the crime shall have been committed, which district shall have been previously ascertained by law."

The Sixth Amendment requirement that courts draw criminal trial juries from the same state and district vicinities in which the crime occurred is known as the "vicinage requirement" and the "Vicinage Clause."[1] This right differs from the Constitution's Article III mandate that all federal criminal jury trials "shall be held in the State where the said Crimes shall have been committed."[2] The Bill of Rights' vicinage guarantee is meant to ensure a jury of one's peers, not a jury trial's location. The Supreme Court has not heard a case about this jury composition right in relation to states and has not incorporated it. However, a lower federal appeals court in *Zicarelli v. Gray* (3d Cir. 1976) assumed that the vicinage right applied at the state level.[3]

1 See *Zicarelli v. Dietz*, 633 F.2d 312, at 314 (3d Cir. 1980).
2 U.S. Constitution, Article III, Section 2.
3 *Zicarelli v. Gray*, 543 F.2d 466 (3d Cir. 1976).

Before *Zicarelli*

The Court broached the Sixth Amendment vicinage requirement while focusing on the timeliness of federal trial proceedings for someone accused of more than one crime in *Beavers v. Haubert* (1905).[4] As long as the federal government held trials in the same federal districts where the crimes were committed, ruled the Court, slowing the process by sequencing or staggering them was not a constitutional issue.[5] Justice Joseph McKenna asserted that "[u]ndoubtedly a defendant is entitled to a speedy trial and by a jury of the district where it is alleged the offense was committed. This is the injunction of the Constitution."[6] He emphasized that a federal trial "must be in the district where the crime was committed" but did not appeal to the Sixth Amendment. The Court in *Ruthenberg v. United States* (1918) held that federal courts did not have to draw juries from all divisions within a district.[7]

The Court suggested in other cases that the vicinage right was already part of the nation's justice system, without stating that it applied to the states. For example, in *Turner v. Louisiana* (1965), which addressed impartial state juries, Justice Potter Stewart referred to the Sixth Amendment sentence that includes the vicinage right, along with speedy, public, and impartial jury trial guarantees, as "the constitutional concept of trial by jury."[8] In *Singer v. United States* (1965), the Court recognized that, like some other criminal trial protections, a defendant in a federal case may voluntarily surrender the vicinage right but not expect the opposite (which would mean relocating the trial to a different state or federal district).[9]

As it had in *Singer*, although with greater attention, the Court in *Duncan v. Louisiana* (1968) explained that the very notion of "jury trial" in the United States included the vicinage right. Some of the evidence that Justice Byron White presented to support jury trial as a fundamental right mentioned vicinage as a necessary aspect of criminal jury trials.[10] The criminal justice system at the federal and state levels has several guarantees, including juries comprised of peers from the defendant's region. However, the Court in *Duncan* only incorporated "jury trial."[11] If it were to ever consider extending the state and district guarantee to the

4 *Beavers v. Haubert*, 198 U.S. 77 (1905).
5 Ibid., at 86.
6 Ibid.
7 *Ruthenberg v. United States*, 245 U.S. 480 (1918).
8 *Turner v. Louisiana*, 379 U.S. 466, at 472 n. 10 (1965).
9 *Singer v. United States*, 380 U.S. 24, at 34, 35 (1965).
10 *Duncan v. Louisiana*, 391 U.S. 145, at 152–54 (1968).
11 Ibid., at 154.

state level, the Court could appeal to the *Duncan* defense of protections that are "fundamental to the American scheme of justice."[12] It could also reference a lower federal court ruling.

Lower federal courts have had a say in this matter, initially affirming that the right did not require state courts to draw juries only from the same state and federal districts of the related crimes. For example, Judge Abraham Lincoln Freedman of the Eastern District of Pennsylvania in *United States v. Nailon* (E.D. Pa. 1962) stated that "[t]he Sixth Amendment guarantees to the accused a trial 'by an impartial jury of the State and district wherein the crime shall have been committed.' This is a limitation, however, upon Federal and not State courts."[13] Circuit Judge Gewin Rives in *Martin v. Beto* (5th Cir. 1968) explained that the Sixth Amendment "right to a trial 'by an impartial jury of the State and district wherein the crime shall have been committed' has not thus far been held applicable to the States."[14] In 1976, however, one federal court ruled differently.

Zicarelli v. Gray (3d Cir. 1976)

In *Zicarelli*, a federal appeals court regarded that the Sixth Amendment vicinage guarantee prevented not just national, but also state government interference. At issue was the state of New Jersey moving a trial to a county in which only one of the several indictments had been filed for the crime of bribing public officials.

Judge Arlin Adams explained in the *Zicarelli* opinion that the Due Process Clause of the Fourteenth Amendment protected any "fundamental" trial right, as the Court ruled in *Duncan*; however, the appeals court was not deciding this status of the Sixth Amendment vicinage right.[15] Nevertheless, "we assume for the purposes of discussion, without expressing any views upon the matter, that the state-and-district guarantee is so closely related to the purpose of the jury trial guarantee that it is applicable to the states."[16]

Reviewing the history of the constitutional vicinage protection, Adams pointed out that "the concept that a criminal trial must be before a jury composed of residents of the county where the crime occurred was not deemed to be of sufficient consequence to be guaranteed by the Constitution."[17] However, "[a]

12 Ibid., at 149.
13 *United States ex rel. Chatary v. Nailon*, 211 F. Supp. 676, at 678 (E.D. Pa. 1962).
14 *Martin v. Beto*, 397 F.2d 741, at 748 (5th Cir. 1968).
15 *Zicarelli*, 543 F.2d 466, at 478–79.
16 Ibid., at 479.
17 Ibid., at 478–79.

defendant may not be tried, over objection, in a federal judicial district other than the one in which the crime was committed."[18] As for the case at hand, "[t]he petit jury was drawn from both the state and the federal judicial district within which the crimes occurred," Adams intoned, "and the state-and-district guarantee of the Constitution promises no more."[19]

Confirmation

In *Zicarelli v. Dietz* (3d Cir. 1980), Judge Dolores Sloviter confirmed that her court in the 1976 *Zicarelli* decision "assumed, without deciding, that the provision of the Sixth Amendment guaranteeing trial before a 'jury of the State and district wherein the crime shall have been committed' is applicable to the states."[20] She also agreed that the federal vicinage right prevented the state from moving a trial to a different federal judicial district but not to a different county.[21] Without citing these cases, another appeals court in *Cook v. Morrill* (5th Cir. 1986) reached the same conclusion, namely, that a state may move a trial within but not outside the federal district in which the associated crime occurred.[22] Judge Frank Johnson in *United States v. Grisham* (11th Cir. 1995) recognized that the Court, in cases like *Ruthenberg*, only required federal courts to determine criminal juries from federal districts.[23]

While a few lower federal courts have assumed that the vicinage right protects a person against state governments, the Court has not yet considered it for incorporation. Nor has it referenced *Zicarelli* in this regard. Occasionally a justice will mention the right when quoting the Sixth Amendment jury trial passage but not in relation to extending it to the state level.[24] "The United States Supreme Court has yet to decide whether the venue provision of the sixth amendment applies to the states," Judge Robert Hill stated in *Cook*.[25] Similarly, the unsigned *Caudill v. Scott* (6th Cir. 1988) opinion explained "that the term 'district' as used in the Sixth Amendment had never been defined to apply to states, that this particular

18 Ibid., at 479.
19 Ibid., at 482.
20 *Zicarelli*, 633 F.2d 312, at 314.
21 Ibid., at 314, 316.
22 *Cook v. Morrill*, 783 F.2d 593, at 596 (5th Cir. 1986).
23 *United States v. Grisham*, 63 F.3d 1074, at 1080 (11th Cir. 1995).
24 See, for example, *Duncan*, 391 U.S. 145, at 153.
25 *Cook*, 783 F.2d 593, at 595.

provision of the Bill of Rights had never been held to have been incorporated into the Fourteenth Amendment."[26]

Summary

The Court has not incorporated the Sixth Amendment right to a jury composed of members from the same state and district of the crime. It has followed the perspective that the jury trial right encompasses specific rights that may include this geographical composition of juries. Yet, it has not decided whether the state and district protection applies at the state level. However, a lower appeals court in the 1976 *Zicarelli* case assumed that this right requires that states select jurors from the district, if not also the state, in which the offense took place. As Adams argued, the vicinage right ensures that a jury is "drawn from both the state and the federal judicial district within which the crimes occurred."[27] If the Court ever hears a case concerning incorporation of this right, it might consider *Zicarelli*.

26 *Caudill v. Scott*, 857 F.2d 344, at 345 (6th Cir. 1988) (*per curiam*).
27 *Zicarelli*, 543 F.2d 466, at 482.

Informed of Accusation

> "In all criminal prosecutions, the accused shall enjoy the right [...] to be informed of the nature and cause of the accusation."

The Sixth Amendment right to be informed of an accusation is also known as "notice of accusation," "notice of charge," "due notice," and simply "notice."[1] This right is similar to the Fifth Amendment protection of grand jury hearings for capital indictments, which the Supreme Court in *Hurtado v. California* (1884) denied as applicable to the states.[2] However, the requirement that government inform the accused of any criminal charge is relevant throughout a prosecution, not just the early indictment phase. The Court regarded notice of accusation as an indispensable element of due process at both state and national levels but did not incorporate it into the Due Process Clause of the Fourteenth Amendment until *Cole v. Arkansas* (1948).[3]

1 See, for example, *Holden v. Hardy*, 169 U.S. 366, at 389–90 (1898); and *In re Oliver*, 333 U.S. 257, at 278 (1948).

2 *Hurtado v. People of California*, 110 U.S. 516 (1884).

3 *Cole v. Arkansas*, 333 U.S. 196 (1948).

Before *Cole*

The Court has long held that federal courts must inform defendants of the government's accusations against them. Initially, it focused on indictments as the mechanism for informing the accused about criminal charges. It held in *United States v. Mills* (1833) and *United States v. Cook* (1872) that federal indictments must provide clear descriptions of accusations.[4] These opinions, however, did not appeal to the Constitution. The Court also considered the indictment process at the state level in *Kennard v. Louisiana* (1876), with Justice Morrison Waite stating that "[a] mere statement of the facts carries with it a complete answer to all the constitutional objections urged against the validity of the act."[5] Yet, he held that the Court had no authority to impose this element of due process of law on states.[6] In *United States v. Cruikshank* (1876), Waite explained that information was the defining feature of indictments at all levels of government because in part it helped check the abuse of government's power.[7] To be informed about the details of an accusation, he emphasized, was "an elementary principle of criminal pleading" and all judges should protect this right, which is not "so granted or secured."[8] Adhering to the *Slaughter-House Cases* (1873) view that state and national civil liberties were distinct, however, the Court could not force states to protect this Sixth Amendment right.[9]

The Court then began to support prosecution by information over formal grand jury indictment procedures. Justice Stanley Matthews in *Hurtado* ruled that a state could pursue criminal prosecutions based on an attorney general's information rather than a grand jury hearing.[10] The Due Process Clause of the Fourteenth Amendment, Matthews argued, meant that states could determine their own judicial procedures; it did not apply Fifth Amendment rights to the states.[11] Justice Henry Brown in *Holden v. Hardy* (1898) affirmed *Hurtado's* ruling in favor of information and argued that due process of law included "certain immutable principles of justice which inhere in the very idea of free government which no member of the Union may disregard."[12]

4 *United States v. Mills*, 32 U.S. (7 Pet.) 138, at 141, 142 (1833); and *United States v. Cook*, 84 U.S. (17 Wall.) 168, at 174 (1872).
5 *Kennard v. Louisiana ex rel. Morgan*, 92 U.S. 480, at 483 (1876).
6 Ibid., at 481.
7 *United States v. Cruikshank*, 92 U.S. 542, at 558 (1876).
8 Ibid., at 558, 559.
9 Ibid., at 549 (citing *Slaughter-House Cases*, 83 U.S. (16 Wall.) 36, at 74 (1873)).
10 *Hurtado*, 110 U.S. 516, at 538.
11 Ibid., at 535.
12 *Holden*, 169 U.S. 366, at 389–90.

For the Court in *Twining v. New Jersey* (1908), *Powell v. Alabama* (1932), *Snyder v. Massachusetts* (1934), and *De Jonge v. Oregon* (1937), due process of law included notice of charge.[13] For instance, Chief Justice Charles Hughes in *De Jonge* asserted that "[c]onviction upon a charge not made would be sheer denial of due process."[14]

In its *In re Oliver* (1948) decision extending the public trial right to the states, the Court presented the right to be informed as already incorporated. It heard *Oliver* nearly two months before *Cole* and announced both decisions on the same day. Justice Hugo Black authored both opinions. He argued that notice of an accusation accompanied several other "basic" criminal trial rights, including public trial, confronting accusatory witnesses, and legal counsel.[15] Justice Wiley Rutledge in his *Oliver* concurrence presented the right to be informed along with other Sixth Amendment rights that also applied at the state level.[16] Neither Black nor Rutledge referenced any incorporation case for this guarantee. The Court had generally taken the right to be informed as part and parcel of due process criminal trial proceedings but had not explicitly incorporated it.

Cole v. Arkansas (1948)

The Court in its unanimous 9-0 *Cole* decision incorporated the right of a defendant to receive information about an accusation. In this case, the Arkansas State Supreme Court upheld the appellants' convictions on a charge that the prosecution in the state trial had not asked the jury to consider. The petitioners argued that this violated their Fourteenth Amendment due process right of knowing the government's accusation against them, in turn denying them a fair trial.[17]

Black explained in the opinion that the issue was that, for the defendants, "it is doubtful both that the information fairly informed them of that charge and that they sought to defend themselves against such a charge."[18] He argued that to be informed of an accusation was an established right of due process of law and therefore applied at the state level. As he explained,

13 *Twining v. State of New Jersey*, 211 U.S. 78, at 111 (1908); *Powell v. Alabama*, 287 U.S. 45, at 68–69 (1932); *Snyder v. Massachusetts*, 291 U.S. 97, at 105 (1934); and *De Jonge v. Oregon*, 299 U.S. 353, at 362 (1937).

14 *De Jonge*, 299 U.S. 353, at 362.

15 *Oliver*, 333 U.S. 257, at 273.

16 Ibid., at 278–79 (Rutledge, J., concurring).

17 *Cole*, 333 U.S. 196, at 197, 200.

18 Ibid., at 201.

> [n]o principle of procedural due process is more clearly established than that notice of the specific charge, and a chance to be heard in a trial of the issues raised by that charge, if desired, are among the constitutional rights of every accused in a criminal proceeding in all courts, state or federal.[19]

The Due Process Clause required government to inform defendants of its criminal accusations against them "in all courts, state or federal." Black cited his *Oliver* opinion for support of this due process protection.[20] On the referenced page in *Oliver*, he defended "the Fourteenth Amendment's guarantee that no one shall be deprived of his liberty without due process of law."[21] Continuing in *Cole*, Black held that "[i]t is as much a violation of due process to send an accused to prison following conviction of a charge on which he was never tried as it would be to convict him upon a charge that was never made."[22] In this case, "the petitioners have been denied safeguards guaranteed by due process of law—safeguards essential to liberty in a government dedicated to justice under law."[23]

Confirmation

For the Court, the right to be informed of an accusation extends to the state level, yet it rarely points to *Cole* as the incorporation case. Black in *Griffin v. Illinois* (1956) cited *Cole* and a few other cases as protecting equal treatment in America's criminal justice system.[24] In *Argersinger v. Hamlin* (1972), Justice William Douglas listed "the right to be informed of the nature and cause of the accusation" along with other due process rights as applying at the state level but did not reference *Cole*.[25]

The lack several *Cole* references may stem from the fact that the state reconsidered and upheld the conviction and, upon another appeal, the Court affirmed the state ruling but on grounds other than state denial of notice of accusation.[26] In *Cole v. Arkansas* (1949), Justice Robert Jackson confirmed that the Court in the earlier *Cole* decision ruled against the state because it relied on "a section of the statute other than that for violation of which these petitioners had been tried

19 Ibid.
20 Ibid. (citing *Oliver*, 333 U.S. 257, at 273).
21 *Oliver*, 333 U.S. 257, at 273.
22 *Cole*, 333 U.S. 196, at 201.
23 Ibid, at 202.
24 *Griffin v. Illinois*, 351 U.S. 12, at 18 (1956).
25 *Argersinger v. Hamlin*, 407 U.S. 25, at 28 (1972).
26 *Cole v. Arkansas*, 338 U.S. 345, at 347, 354 (1949).

and convicted."[27] Now, however, the state had adequately addressed that issue, and the appeal was focusing on other aspects of the convictions.

The Court has also acknowledged elsewhere that in the 1948 *Cole* decision it applied the right to be informed of an accusation to the state level. It has appealed to Black's argument in *Cole* that the Due Process Clause protects against conviction based "upon a charge that was never made." This included Chief Justice Earl Warren ruling in *Garner v. Louisiana* (1961) against a state's convictions because of a lack of evidence, which he argued was like convicting someone "for a charge that was never made," for which he referenced *Cole*.[28] The Court quoted *Cole* in its unsigned *Rabe v. Washington* (1972) opinion to support its reversal of a state's conviction of a person that was "affirmed under a statute with a meaning quite different from the one he was charged with violating."[29] Warren in his *Estes v. Texas* (1965) concurrence made a clear confirmation, explaining "that the fundamental conception of a fair trial includes many of the specific provisions of the Sixth Amendment, such as [...] the right to notice of specific charges, *Cole v. Arkansas*."[30] Justices have not credited any other case in which the Court extended the due notice right to the states.

As with other criminal trial rights, many justices may regard the right of a defendant to be informed of an accusation as so integral to the justice system that they often include it among other due process rights. Some justices have asserted that the Court has incorporated all Sixth Amendment rights including notice of charge.[31]

Summary

The Court in *Cole* incorporated the Sixth Amendment right to be informed of an accusation. Black explained that "notice of the specific charge" is "among the constitutional rights of every accused in a criminal proceeding in all courts, state or federal."[32] A few justices have confirmed *Cole* as the incorporation case for this right.

27 Ibid., at 347.
28 *Garner v. Louisiana*, 368 U.S. 157, at 164 n. 10 (1961).
29 *Rabe v. Washington*, 405 U.S. 313, at 314 (1972) (*per curiam*).
30 *Estes v. Texas*, 381 U.S. 532, at 560 (1965) (Warren, E., concurring).
31 See, for example, *Faretta v. California*, 422 U.S. 806, at 818 (1975).
32 *Cole*, 333 U.S. 196, at 201.

Confront Witnesses

"In all criminal prosecutions, the accused shall enjoy the right [...] to be confronted with the witnesses against him."

The Supreme Court refers to the Sixth Amendment right of the accused to confront an opposing witness as the "Confrontation Clause" and regards cross-examination as the primary way of ensuring this guarantee.[1] The Court in *Pointer v. Texas* (1965) incorporated the Sixth Amendment right to confront adversarial witnesses.

Before *Pointer*

The Court initially held that the right to confront prosecution witnesses did not extend to the states. For example, Justice Rufus Peckham in *West v. Louisiana* (1904) explained that, "[a]s the Sixth Amendment does not apply to state courts, the question as to what is required under its provisions in order to preserve the right to be confronted with the witness is eliminated from any inquiry by this Court."[2]

1 See, for example, *Dowdell v. United States*, 221 U.S. 325, at 330 (1911); *Pointer v. Texas*, 380 U.S. 400, at 404–5 (1965); *Douglas v. Alabama*, 380 U.S. 415, at 418 (1965); and *Faretta v. California*, 422 U.S. 806, at 816 (1975).

2 *West v. Louisiana*, 194 U.S. 258, at 264 (1904).

Chief Justice William Taft in *Gaines v. Washington* (1928) did not mention confrontation but asserted that "the Sixth Amendment to the Federal Constitution does not apply to the trial of criminal prosecutions by a state."[3]

In a 5-4 decision, the Court in *Snyder v. Massachusetts* (1934) ruled against applying the confrontation right to the state level. Authoring the *Snyder* opinion, Justice Benjamin Cardozo held that each state had autonomy over its trial procedures "in accordance with its own conception of policy and fairness, unless in so doing it offends some principle of justice so rooted in the traditions and conscience of our people as to be ranked as fundamental."[4] At that time, the Court did not see confronting an accusatory witness as fundamental. Cardozo concluded that

> the privilege to confront one's accusers and cross-examine them face to face is assured to a defendant by the Sixth Amendment in prosecutions in the federal courts (*Gaines v. Washington*), and in prosecutions in the state courts is assured very often by the Constitutions of the states.[5]

In some later decisions, however, the Court included confrontation along with other criminal trial guarantees. For Justice Hugo Black in *In re Oliver* (1948), a defendant had "a right to examine the witnesses against him."[6] A few months before *Pointer*, the Court announced in *Singer v. United States* (1965) that, like most other constitutional trial rights, a defendant may waive the right of confrontation but could not "insist upon the opposite of that right."[7]

The Court brought some fundamental criminal trial rights into the Due Process Clause before *Pointer*, protecting them from state infringement. These included the Fifth Amendment right against compulsory self-incrimination in *Malloy v. Hogan* (1964) and Sixth Amendment rights to notice of charge in *Cole v. Arkansas* (1948), public trial in *Oliver*, and counsel for felony charges in *Gideon v. Wainwright* (1963).[8]

3 *Gaines v. Washington*, 277 U.S. 81, at 85 (1928).
4 *Snyder v. Massachusetts*, 291 U.S. 97, at 105 (1934).
5 Ibid., at 106 (citation information omitted).
6 *In re Oliver*, 333 U.S. 257, at 273 (1948).
7 *Singer v. United States*, 380 U.S. 24, at 34–35 (1965).
8 *Malloy v. Hogan*, 378 U.S. 1 (1964); *Cole v. Arkansas*, 333 U.S. 196 (1948); *Oliver*, 333 U.S. 257; and *Gideon v. Wainwright*, 372 U.S. 335 (1963).

Pointer v. Texas (1965)

The 9-0 *Pointer* ruling incorporated the Sixth Amendment right to confront an opposing witness. In this case, the defendant was unable to cross-examine a prosecution witness because the state court only provided the transcript of the testimony. While the justices disputed incorporation theory, they supported the right of a defendant to confront accusatory witnesses at the state level. Black reviewed the recent incorporation arguments of *Gideon* and *Malloy* that the Fourteenth Amendment protected Bill of Rights' guarantees that are "'fundamental and essential to a fair trial.'"[9] He made the *Pointer* ruling clear, stating that "[w]e hold today that the Sixth Amendment's right of an accused to confront the witnesses against him is likewise a fundamental right and is made obligatory on the States by the Fourteenth Amendment."[10]

The Court held that several previous rulings and the text of the Sixth Amendment identified this right as "fundamental" for a "fair trial."[11] For example, Black argued "that the right of confrontation and cross-examination is an essential and fundamental requirement for the kind of fair trial which is this country's constitutional goal."[12] He included *Oliver* prominently among the cases he referenced to support the Court's holding "that to deprive an accused of the right to cross-examine the witnesses against him is a denial of the Fourteenth Amendment's guarantee of due process of law."[13] Following *Gideon* and *Malloy*, Black asserted that "it no longer can broadly be said that the Sixth Amendment does not apply to state courts," and "[w]e hold that petitioner was entitled to be tried in accordance with the protection of the confrontation guarantee of the Sixth Amendment."[14] Additionally, Black followed the *Malloy* standard, explaining that the confrontation right, "like the right against compelled self-incrimination, is 'to be enforced against the States under the Fourteenth Amendment according to the same standards that protect those personal rights against federal encroachment.'"[15] The three separate concurring opinions agreed with the ruling of the Court but not with its rationale. Justice John Harlan II, for example, argued that the Court

9 *Pointer*, 380 U.S. 400, at 403 (quoting *Gideon*, 372 U.S. 335, at 342; and *Malloy*, 378 U.S. 1, at 6).
10 *Pointer*, 380 U.S. 400, at 403.
11 Ibid., at 404–6.
12 Ibid., at 405.
13 Ibid.
14 Ibid., at 406.
15 Ibid. (quoting *Malloy*, 378 U.S. 1, at 10).

should instead follow the *Palko* ordered liberty approach to protect federal rights against state invasion.[16]

Confirmation

Justices have made a few ambiguous references about the Court's extension of the Confrontation Clause to the state level. For example, Justice Arthur Goldberg in *Griswold v. Connecticut* (1965) noted *Pointer* along with a few other incorporation cases when explaining that "[t]his Court, in a series of decisions, has held that the Fourteenth Amendment absorbs and applies to the States those specifics of the first eight amendments which express fundamental personal rights."[17] He did not identify which case protected which right, however. Chief Justice Earl Warren in his *Estes v. Texas* (1965) concurrence identified both *Pointer* and *Douglas v. Alabama* (1965) for protecting confrontation in state prosecution trials.[18]

In contrast to these few indistinct references, justices have often recognized that the Court in *Pointer* incorporated the confrontation right. In arguing that cross-examination satisfied the right of confrontation, Justice William Brennan stated at the beginning of *Douglas* that "the Confrontation Clause of the Sixth Amendment is applicable to the States. *Pointer v. Texas*."[19] He reaffirmed this years later in *Lee v. Illinois* (1986).[20] Warren was more specific in *Washington v. Texas* (1967) than he had been in *Estes*, now only citing *Pointer* for incorporating the right.[21] Other justices crediting *Pointer* as the incorporation case for the confrontation right include Justice Byron White in *Duncan v. Louisiana* (1968), Black in *Illinois v. Allen* (1970), Douglas in *Argersinger v. Hamlin* (1972), Chief Justice Warren Burger in *Davis v. Alaska* (1974), Justice Potter Stewart in *Faretta v. California* (1975), Justice Lewis Powell in *Pennsylvania v. Ritchie* (1987), Justice Samuel Alito in *McDonald v. Chicago* (2010), and Justice Antonin Scalia in *Crawford v. Washington* (2004).[22]

16 *Pointer*, 380 U.S. 400, at 408–9 (Harlan, J., concurring).
17 *Griswold v. Connecticut*, 381 U.S. 479, at 488 n. 2 (1965) (Goldberg, A., concurring).
18 *Estes v. Texas*, 381 U.S. 532, at 560 (1965) (Warren, E., concurring).
19 *Douglas*, 380 U.S. 415, at 418 (citation information omitted).
20 *Lee v. Illinois*, 476 U.S. 530, at 539 (1986).
21 *Washington v. Texas*, 388 U.S. 14, at 18 n. 9 (1967).
22 *Duncan v. Louisiana*, 391 U.S. 145, at 148 n. 11 (1968); *Illinois v. Allen*, 397 U.S. 337, at 338 (1970); *Argersinger v. Hamlin*, 407 U.S. 25, at 27–28 (1972); *Davis v. Alaska*, 415 U.S. 308, at 315 (1974); *Faretta*, 422 U.S. 806, at 818 n. 14; *Pennsylvania v. Ritchie*, 480 U.S. 39, at 45 n. 5 (1987); *McDonald v. City of Chicago*, 561 U.S. 742, at 764 n. 12 (2010); and *Crawford v. Washington*, 541 U.S. 36, at 42 (2004).

Summary

In *Pointer*, the Court incorporated the right to confront an oppositional witness. As Black held, "the Sixth Amendment's right of an accused to confront the witnesses against him [...] is made obligatory on the States by the Fourteenth Amendment."[23] In addition to this stout incorporation statement, the Court has confirmed this development several times.

23 *Pointer*, 380 U.S. 400, at 403.

Favorable Witnesses

> "In all criminal prosecutions, the accused shall enjoy the right [...] to have compulsory process for obtaining witnesses in his favor."

The Supreme Court in *Washington v. Texas* (1967) extended the Sixth Amendment right to obtain a favorable witness to the state level.[1] This compulsory process guarantee—also known as the "Compulsory Process Clause"—is associated with the right to confront opposing witnesses, which the Court incorporated in *Pointer v. Texas* (1965).[2] The Court regards both rights, along with others, including informed of an accusation, public trial, and speedy trial, as necessary for a person accused of a crime to present a defense.[3]

Before *Washington*

Prior to *Washington*, it was not unusual for justices to leave the compulsory defense witness guarantee off their lists of Sixth Amendment rights.[4] Justice Hugo Black,

1 *Washington v. Texas*, 388 U.S. 14 (1967).
2 *Pointer v. Texas*, 380 U.S. 400 (1965).
3 See *In re Oliver*, 333 U.S. 257, at 273 (1948); and *In re Murchison*, 349 U.S. 133, at 134 (1955).
4 See, for example, *Snyder v. Massachusetts*, 291 U.S. 97, at 129–30 (1934) (Roberts, O., dissenting).

however, included the favorable witness right along with other trial protections. He explained in the *In re Oliver* (1948) opinion that due process of law required that, along with other criminal trial protections, a defendant has the right to "call other witnesses in his behalf, either by way of defense or explanation."[5] In the *In re Murchison* (1955) opinion, Black reiterated that "due process requires, as a minimum, that an accused be given a public trial after reasonable notice of the charges, have a right to examine witnesses against him, call witnesses on his own behalf, and be represented by counsel."[6] While Black in these cases mentioned the defense witness right, he did not consider whether it applied at the state level.

During the early- to mid-1960s, the Court incorporated several criminal trial rights, including the Fifth Amendment right against compulsory self-incrimination and Sixth Amendment rights to counsel for capital accusations, confrontation of opposing witnesses, and impartial jury trials.[7] It defended doing so with the general argument that these protections were necessary for due process of law, and therefore the Due Process Clause of the Fourteenth Amendment included them in its broad protection against state abridgment.[8]

Washington v. Texas (1967)

The Court in *Washington* ruled that the Due Process Clause protected a compulsory favorable witness process at all levels of government because the right was necessary for fair trials.[9] This case concerned Texas state laws that prevented co-participants in an alleged crime from testifying on behalf of each other. Chief Justice Earl Warren, authoring the 9-0 *Washington* opinion, explained that

> [w]e have not previously been called upon to decide whether the right of an accused to have compulsory process for obtaining witnesses in his favor, guaranteed in federal trials by the Sixth Amendment, is so fundamental and essential to a fair trial that it is incorporated in the Due Process Clause of the Fourteenth Amendment.[10]

5 *Oliver*, 333 U.S. 257, at 275, see also 273.
6 *Murchison*, 349 U.S. 133, at 134.
7 *Malloy v. Hogan*, 378 U.S. 1 (1964) (no self-incrimination); *Gideon v. Wainwright*, 372 U.S. 335 (1963) (counsel); *Pointer*, 380 U.S. 400 (confrontation); and *Parker v. Gladden*, 385 U.S. 363 (1966) (impartial jury).
8 See *Estes v. Texas*, 381 U.S. 532, at 559–60 (1965) (Warren, E., concurring).
9 *Washington*, 388 U.S. 14, at 17–18, see also 15 n. 2.
10 Ibid., at 17–18.

He cited *Gideon v. Wainwright* (1963) for this rationale, which posited that "a provision of the Bill of Rights which is 'fundamental and essential to a fair trial' is made obligatory upon the States by the Fourteenth Amendment."[11]

Warren elaborated that "in recent years we have increasingly looked to the specific guarantees of the Sixth Amendment to determine whether a state criminal trial was conducted with due process of law."[12] This meant that the Court was moving away from trying to make judgments as to whether a state violation was "shocking," not "rooted in the traditions," or jeopardized "ordered liberty" to justify using the Fourteenth Amendment to protect a federal right, as it initially put forward in *Snyder v. Massachusetts* (1934) and *Palko v. Connecticut* (1937).[13] Instead, Warren placed the favorable witness guarantee alongside other fundamental rights of due process of law that the Court had already incorporated. He held that "[t]he right of an accused to have compulsory process for obtaining witnesses in his favor stands on no lesser footing than the other Sixth Amendment rights that we have previously held applicable to the States."[14] Due process of law in the criminal justice system necessarily required several rights, including defense witnesses. He referenced *Oliver* as providing a similar description.

Someone accused of a crime cannot have a constitutionally valid defense without a supporting witness. As Warren summarized, "[t]he right to offer the testimony of witnesses, and to compel their attendance, if necessary, is in plain terms, the right to present a defense."[15] As with other incorporated Sixth Amendment rights, the accused "has the right to present his own witnesses to establish a defense. This right is a fundamental element of due process of law."[16] A state could not "prevent whole categories of defense witnesses from testifying on the basis of *a priori* categories that presume them unworthy of belief."[17] This included accomplices who would presumably lie under oath.

Confirmation

The Court has stated more than once that in *Washington* it extended the right of a compulsory defense witness process to the state level. Occasionally, a

11 Ibid., at 18 n. 6 (quoting *Gideon*, 372 U.S. 335, at 342).
12 *Washington*, 388 U.S. 14, at 18.
13 *Snyder*, 291 U.S. 97, at 105; and *Palko v. Connecticut*, 302 U.S. 319, at 325, 328 (1937).
14 *Washington*, 388 U.S. 14, at 18.
15 Ibid., at 19.
16 Ibid.
17 Ibid., at 22 (emphasis in original).

justice is unclear about this. For example, Justice Sandra Day O'Connor in *Crane v. Kentucky* (1986) wrote "the Compulsory Process or Confrontation clauses of the Sixth Amendment, *Washington v. Texas* (1967)" without distinguishing which of these two rights the case protected.[18] The Court in *Webb v. Texas* (1972) favorably quoted a passage from *Washington* but not in reference to it applying the favorable witness right to the states.[19] Such ambiguous descriptions about this incorporation case, however, are few.

More common are acknowledgments that *Washington* is the defense witness incorporation case. For example, the Court stated in *Cool v. United States* (1972) that "[i]n *Washington v. Texas*, we held that a criminal defendant has a Sixth Amendment right to present to the jury exculpatory testimony of an accomplice."[20] Various justices have recognized that the Court in *Washington* protected the defense witness right against states, including Justice Byron White in *Duncan v. Louisiana* (1968), Justice William Douglas in *Argersinger v. Hamlin* (1972), Justice Potter Stewart in *Faretta v. California* (1975), Justice Lewis Powell in *Pennsylvania v. Ritchie* (1987), and Chief Justice William Rehnquist in *Albright v. Oliver* (1994).[21] Justice Samuel Alito's identification of the case in *McDonald v. Chicago* (2010) is typical of these brief confirmations. In a footnote listing several incorporation cases and attending rights, he included "*Washington v. Texas* (1967) (compulsory process)."[22]

Summary

The Court in *Washington* incorporated the Sixth Amendment right to a favorable witness. "The right of an accused to have compulsory process for obtaining witnesses in his favor," Warren asserted, is "held applicable to the States."[23] The Court has subsequently referenced *Washington* several times as the case in which it applied the defense witness protection to the state level.

18 *Crane v. Kentucky*, 476 U.S. 683, at 690 (1986) (citation information omitted).

19 *Webb v. Texas*, 409 U.S. 95, at 98 (1972) (*per curiam*).

20 *Cool v. United States*, 409 U.S. 100, at 104 (1972) (*per curiam*; citation information omitted).

21 *Duncan v. Louisiana*, 391 U.S. 145, at 148 n. 12 (1968); *Argersinger v. Hamlin*, 407 U.S. 25, at 27–28 (1972); *Faretta v. California*, 422 U.S. 806, at 818 n. 14 (1975); *Pennsylvania v. Ritchie*, 480 U.S. 39, at 45 n. 5 (1987); and *Albright v. Oliver*, 510 U.S. 266, at 273 (1994).

22 *McDonald v. City of Chicago*, 561 U.S. 742, at 764 n. 12 (2010).

23 *Washington*, 388 U.S. 14, at 18.

Counsel

> "In all criminal prosecutions, the accused shall enjoy the right [...] to have the Assistance of Counsel for his defence."

The Supreme Court protected the Sixth Amendment right to counsel from state denial in more than one case as it considered different crimes and punishments, expanding the guarantee to the most people in *Gideon v. Wainwright* (1963).[1] It initially incorporated the right in *Powell v. Alabama* (1932); however, this ruling only applied to defendants facing the death penalty.[2] The Court reversed itself in *Betts v. Brady* (1942), holding that the right to counsel did not extend to the states but it could in some circumstances.[3] Returning to counsel in *Gideon*, the Court overturned *Betts* and ruled that the right covered anyone accused of a felony, not just a capital offense.

1 *Gideon v. Wainwright*, 372 U.S. 335 (1963).
2 *Powell v. Alabama*, 287 U.S. 45 (1932).
3 *Betts v. Brady*, 316 U.S. 455 (1942).

Before *Gideon*

While most state constitutions and judicial rulings protected the right to counsel for criminal defendants, state trial judges would instead regularly favor expeditious trial proceedings.[4] In *Holden v. Hardy* (1898), the Court mentioned that unlike England, American colonies guaranteed fair trial rights, including counsel for serious crimes.[5] The Court did not consider application of this Sixth Amendment right to the state level until *Powell*.[6] It did, however, develop a rationale for protecting federal rights against state abridgment.

The Court in different decisions formulated a due process defense of fundamental rights before *Powell* and *Gideon*. Justice John Harlan in his *Hurtado v. California* (1884) dissent argued that "due process of law protects the fundamental principles of liberty and justice."[7] The Court in *Chicago, Burlington & Quincy Railroad v. Chicago* (1897) appealed to the Due Process Clause of the Fourteenth Amendment to extend the Fifth Amendment right of just compensation to the state level.[8] In *Twining v. New Jersey* (1908) it defended using the Due Process Clause to protect "fundamental rights."[9] In *Gitlow v. New York* (1925) it did just that by incorporating free speech and suggesting that the Court could extend other federal rights.[10] The Court also discussed this due process defense of fundamental rights in *Hebert v. Louisiana* (1926) and *Stromberg v. California* (1931).[11] Chief Justice Charles Hughes in *Near v. Minnesota* (1931) followed the same rationale to incorporate free press.[12]

In *Powell*, the Court held that the right to counsel applied in capital cases at the state level for defendants who could not obtain their own defense attorneys. Justice George Sutherland reviewed the Court's history of using the Fourteenth Amendment Due Process Clause to incorporate "fundamental rights," including in *Gitlow* and *Near*.[13] Without ruling against the Court's refusal in *Hurtado* to

4 *Powell*, 287 U.S. 45, at 56–61.

5 *Holden v. Hardy*, 169 U.S. 366, at 386 (1898); see also *Powell*, 287 U.S. 45, at 60–65.

6 *Powell*, 287 U.S. 45, at 68.

7 *Hurtado v. People of California*, 110 U.S. 516, at 558 (1884).

8 *Chicago, Burlington & Quincy Railroad Co. v. Chicago*, 166 U.S. 226, at 236 (1897).

9 *Twining v. State of New Jersey*, 211 U.S. 78, at 99–100, 101, 106, 107 (1908).

10 *Gitlow v. People of New York*, 268 U.S. 652, at 666 (1925).

11 *Hebert v. Louisiana*, 272 U.S. 312, at 316 (1926); and *Stromberg v. California*, 283 U.S. 359, at 368 (1931).

12 *Near v. State of Minnesota ex rel. Olson*, 283 U.S. 697, at 707 (1931).

13 *Powell*, 287 U.S. 45, at 66–68. He explained that the Court established this incorporation rationale in various cases, including *Twining*, 211 U.S. 78, at 99; *Gitlow*, 268 U.S. 652, at 666; *Hebert*, 272 U.S. 312, at 316; *Stromberg*, 283 U.S. 359, at 368; and *Near*, 283 U.S. 697, at 707.

extend the grand jury right to the state level, Sutherland asserted that the Court's incorporation of just compensation, speech, and press showed that, "notwithstanding the sweeping character of the language in the *Hurtado* case, the rule laid down is not without exceptions."[14] Like free speech and press, he argued that the right of counsel "is of such a character that it cannot be denied without violating those 'fundamental principles of liberty and justice which lie at the base of all our civil and political institutions,'" using a phrase from *Hebert*.[15] Sutherland held that legal counsel was among other necessary criminal justice procedures, including "notice and hearing," that "constitute basic elements of the constitutional requirement of due process of law."[16] Yet, Sutherland's defense of legal counsel in *Powell* only concerned defendants charged with capital crimes who were unable to secure an attorney for reasons outside of their control, including "ignorance, feeble mindedness, illiteracy, or the like."[17] At both federal and state levels, it is "the duty of the trial judge, where the accused is unable to employ counsel, to appoint counsel for him," Sutherland ruled.[18] He clarified, however, "at least in cases like the present."[19]

When returning to the issue of the right of counsel at the state level a decade later, the Court in *Betts* ruled against incorporating it for situations involving indigent persons accused of crimes less serious than murder or rape.[20] Justice Owen Roberts argued that "[t]he Sixth Amendment of the national Constitution applies only to trials in federal courts. The due process clause of the Fourteenth Amendment does not incorporate, as such, the specific guarantees found in the Sixth Amendment."[21] However, Roberts explained that state infringement of criminal trial rights "may, in one setting, constitute a denial of fundamental fairness, shocking to the universal sense of justice, may, in other circumstances and in the light of other considerations, fall short of such denial."[22] Among the several cases he cited to support his contingent incorporation approach were *Hurtado*, *Twining*, *Powell*, and *Palko v. Connecticut* (1937).[23] For the Court majority in *Betts*,

14 *Powell*, 287 U.S. 45, at 67 (citing *Hurtado*, 110 U.S. 516).
15 *Powell*, 287 U.S. 45, at 67 (quoting *Hebert*, 272 U.S. 312, at 316).
16 *Powell*, 287 U.S. 45, at 68.
17 Ibid., at 71.
18 Ibid., at 73.
19 Ibid.
20 *Betts*, 316 U.S. 455, at 457.
21 Ibid., at 461–62, see also 471.
22 Ibid., at 462.
23 Ibid., at 462 n. 10, 11 (citing *Hurtado,* 110 U.S. 516; *Twining,* 211 U.S. 78; *Powell,* 287 U.S. 45; and *Palko v. Connecticut,* 302 U.S. 319 (1937)).

the state denial of counsel for the indigent did not violate "fundamental fairness" or shock "the universal sense of justice," and therefore was not constitutionally invalid.

Gideon v. Wainwright (1963)

In a 9-0 vote, the Court in *Gideon* overturned *Betts* and used a familiar rationale to expand the right of counsel to include indigent defendants facing non-capital yet series criminal accusations. This case addressed a Florida law that provided legal counsel only to those accused of capital crimes who could not afford an attorney. The statute did not cover defendants facing possible misdemeanor and felony charges, regardless of the severity of the possible punishment. The Court in *Gideon* ruled that the Due Process Clause of the Fourteenth Amendment protected the Sixth Amendment right to legal counsel at the state level for anyone accused of a serious offense who was unable to pay for legal representation.

Borrowing a phrase from *Betts*, Justice Hugo Black asserted that legal counsel is "a fundamental right, essential to a fair trial."[24] Unfortunately, the Court in that case had not regarded counsel for indigent criminal defendants as fundamental.[25] He vindicated *Powell* as having it right all along, explaining that

> those guarantees of the Bill of Rights which are fundamental safeguards of liberty immune from federal abridgment are equally protected against state invasion by the Due Process Clause of the Fourteenth Amendment. This same principle was recognized, explained, and applied in *Powell v. Alabama*.[26]

The Court in *Powell* held that the Due Process Clause incorporated the fundamental right of counsel but only for a narrow range of cases. Black elaborated that *Powell's* "conclusions about the fundamental nature of the right to counsel are unmistakable"; however, he cautioned that "the Court at the close of its *Powell* opinion did by its language, as this Court frequently does, limit its holding to the particular facts and circumstances of that case."[27]

In agreement with the some of the *Betts* incorporation rationale, Black explained "that a provision of the Bill of Rights which is 'fundamental and essential to a fair trial' is made obligatory upon the States by the Fourteenth Amendment."[28]

24 *Gideon*, 372 U.S. 335, at 339 (quoting *Betts*, 316 U.S. 455, at 471).
25 *Gideon*, 372 U.S. 335, at 340.
26 Ibid., at 341.
27 Ibid., at 343.
28 Ibid., at 342 (quoting *Betts*, 316 U.S. 455, at 465).

"We think the Court in *Betts* was wrong, however," Black stated, "in concluding that the Sixth Amendment's guarantee of counsel is not one of these fundamental rights."[29] Various decisions, he explained, including *Powell*, *Grosjean v. American Press* (1936), and *Johnson v. Zerbst* (1938) regarded legal counsel as a "fundamental right."[30] "[T]he Court in *Betts v. Brady* made an abrupt break with its own well-considered precedents. In returning to these old precedents," continued Black, "sounder we believe than the new, we but restore constitutional principles established to achieve a fair system of justice."[31] As legal representation was a fundamental right, "in our adversary system of criminal justice, any person haled into court, who is too poor to hire a lawyer, cannot be assured a fair trial unless counsel is provided for him."[32] He emphasized that "[t]he right of one charged with crime to counsel may not be deemed fundamental and essential to fair trials in some countries, but it is in ours."

Confirmation

The Court has recognized *Gideon* as the counsel incorporation decision more often than it has *Powell*. Returning to the author of the 1932 opinion, Sutherland stated in *Grosjean* that the Court in *Powell* protected "the fundamental right of the accused to the aid of counsel in a criminal prosecution" against states.[33] The few other citations to *Powell* regarding incorporation of counsel are diluted with multiple case references. For example, in *Argersinger v. Hamlin* (1972)—in which the majority protected counsel for defendants facing imprisonment regardless of the offense—Justice William Douglas elaborated that, following *Powell* and other cases including *Gideon*, "fundamental" rights like counsel are necessary for a "fair trial."[34] Justice Potter Stewart in *Faretta v. California* (1975) also referenced several cases as having brought the right of counsel to the states, including *Powell* and *Gideon*.[35] Chief Justice Warren Burger in *Wainwright v. Sykes* (1977) stated that both *Argersinger* and *Gideon* held "that every defendant who faces the possibility

29 *Gideon*, 372 U.S. 335, at 342.

30 Ibid., at 343 (citing *Powell*, 287 U.S. 45, at 68; *Grosjean v. American Press Co., Inc.*, 297 U.S. 233, at 243–44 (1936); and *Johnson v. Zerbst*, 304 U.S. 458, at 462 (1938)).

31 *Gideon*, 372 U.S. 335, at 344.

32 Ibid.

33 *Grosjean*, 297 U.S. 233, at 243–44.

34 *Argersinger v. Hamlin*, 407 U.S. 25, at 31–33 (1972).

35 *Faretta v. California*, 422 U.S. 806, at 832 (1975).

of incarceration be afforded counsel."[36] The Court understands that *Powell* applied the right only to capital cases.[37] Otherwise, it ignores *Powell* as the counsel incorporation case.

Several justices have referred specifically to *Gideon* as the case in which the Court incorporated the right to counsel. Black in *Pointer v. Texas* (1965) asserted that "in *Gideon v. Wainwright*, we held that the Fourteenth Amendment makes the Sixth Amendment's guarantee of right to counsel obligatory upon the States."[38] He also mentioned this development in his *Griswold v. Connecticut* (1965) dissent.[39] Justice William Brennan in *Malloy v. Hogan* (1964), Chief Justice Earl Warren in *Estes v. Texas* (1965) and *Washington v. Texas* (1967), Justice Thurgood Marshall in *Mempa v. Rhay* (1967), Justice Byron White in *Duncan v. Louisiana* (1968), Justice John Harlan II in his *Duncan* dissent, Chief Justice William Rehnquist in *Albright v. Oliver* (1994), and Justice Samuel Alito in *McDonald v. Chicago* (2010) each confirmed *Gideon* as extending the right of counsel to the state level.[40]

Summary

The Court incorporated the right to counsel in *Gideon*, providing coverage for anyone accused of a serious crime who cannot afford an attorney. This was more comprehensive than the *Powell* ruling, which only applied the counsel guarantee to those accused of capitol offences. In *Betts*, the Court did not go any further with the right. In *Gideon*, it overruled *Betts* and appealed to the due process protection of fundamental rights to ensure legal representation at the state level for most defendants. Black argued that the right to counsel was a fundamental right and, as such, "is made obligatory upon the States by the Fourteenth Amendment."[41] Justices have often credited *Gideon* as the counsel incorporation case.

36 *Wainwright v. Sykes*, 433 U.S. 72, at 93 (1977) (Burger, W., concurring; citation information omitted).

37 See, for example, *Gideon*, 372 U.S. 335, at 341; and *Malloy v. Hogan*, 378 U.S. 1, at 6 (1964).

38 *Pointer v. Texas*, 380 U.S. 400, at 401 (1965) (citation information omitted).

39 *Griswold v. Connecticut*, 381 U.S. 479, at 526 n. 21 (1965) (Black, H., dissenting).

40 *Malloy*, 378 U.S. 1, at 10; *Estes v. Texas*, 381 U.S. 532, at 560 (1965) (Warren, E., concurring); *Washington v. Texas*, 388 U.S. 14, at 18 n. 8 (1967); *Mempa v. Rhay*, 389 U.S. 128, at 134 (1967); *Duncan v. Louisiana*, 391 U.S. 145, at 148 n. 8; 179 n. 14 (Harlan, J., dissenting) (1968); *Albright v. Oliver*, 510 U.S. 266, at 273 (1994); and *McDonald v. City of Chicago*, 561 U.S. 742, at 764 n. 12 (2010).

41 *Gideon*, 372 U.S. 335, at 342 (quoting *Betts*, 316 U.S. 455, at 465).

PART VII

SEVENTH AMENDMENT

Civil Jury Trial

> "In Suits at common law, where the value in controversy shall exceed twenty dollars, the right of trial by jury shall be preserved."

The Seventh Amendment covers civil jury trials, which seek damages rather than injunctive relief. As Justice Joseph Story described in 1830, the amendment is about "the right of trial by jury in civil cases."[1] Both before and after ratification of the Fourteenth Amendment, the Supreme Court asserted that the right to civil jury trials only pertained to the federal government. In *Walker v. Sauvinet* (1876), it ruled that the Fourteenth Amendment did not protect the civil jury right against state governments.[2]

Before *Walker*

As soon as the Court considered the Seventh Amendment, it held that its guarantees applied only to the federal level. In *Parsons v. Bedford* (1830), Story held that both clauses of the amendment regarded civil law suits in federal courts.[3]

1 *Parsons v. Bedford*, 28 U.S. (3 Pet.) 433, at 446 (1830).
2 *Walker v. Sauvinet*, 92 U.S. 90, at 92 (1876).
3 *Parsons*, 28 U.S. 433, at 446.

He also distinguished the two rights of the amendment, a view justices have since followed.[4] Story pointed out that the 1789 Judiciary Act protected jury trials in all federal courts for "issues in fact."[5] He did not mention the $20 threshold.

In *Barron v. Baltimore* (1833), the Court held that the Bill of Rights did not concern states, a view it followed for decades.[6] As Chief Justice John Marshall in *Barron* stated in reference to the Bill of Rights, "[t]hese amendments contain no expression indicating an intention to apply them to the state governments. This court cannot so apply them."[7]

However, the Fourteenth Amendment that states ratified in 1868 protected privileges and immunities, due process of law, and equality under the law against state infringement. The amendment prefaced these guarantees with "[n]o state shall," clearly distinguishing them as applying to the state level. This addition to the Constitution carried the potential to alter the Court's *Barron* perspective of the Bill of Rights, including the Seventh Amendment.

Justice Samuel Nelson in *Justices v. Murray* (1870) held that the right to a civil jury trial for property damages only related to federal courts.[8] For him, "common law" in America meant that federal and state governments had discretion over their respective civil jury trials, regardless of how much money was involved.[9] Moreover, the Court ruled in *Barron* that the Bill of Rights' protections "are limitations upon the powers of the Federal government, and not upon the States."[10] Therefore, he concluded, "according to the construction uniformly given to the first clause of this amendment, the suits there mentioned are confined to those in the Federal courts."[11] Nelson did not mention the Fourteenth Amendment or due process.

Similarly, Justice Nathan Clifford in *Edwards v. Elliott* (1874) asserted that the civil jury right "does not apply to trials in the state courts" without any explanation or reference to previous rulings addressing the Seventh Amendment.[12] He did, however, cite *Barron* to support this view.[13] Like Nelson in *Justices*, Clifford did not appeal to due process of law or the Fourteenth Amendment.

4 Ibid., at 447.
5 Ibid.
6 *Barron ex rel. Tiernan v. City of Baltimore*, 32 U.S. (7 Pet.) 243 (1833).
7 Ibid., at 250.
8 *The Justices v. Murray*, 76 U.S. (9 Wall.) 274 (1870).
9 Ibid., at 277–79.
10 Ibid., at 278 (citing *Barron*, 32 U.S. 243).
11 *Justices*, 76 U.S. 274, at 277.
12 *Edwards v. Elliott*, 88 U.S. (21 Wall.) 532, at 557 (1874).
13 Ibid., at 557 n. 17 (citing *Barron*, 32 U.S. 243, at 247).

Walker v. Sauvinet (1876)

In its 7-2 *Walker* decision, the Court did not deviate from its earlier position that the right to civil jury trials only related to federal courts.[14] It did, however, integrate the Fourteenth Amendment into its defense of the right's inapplicability to the state level. The case regarded a Louisiana law permitting judges to rule in non-criminal cases if juries could not reach verdicts.

Referencing *Edwards*, Justice Morrison Waite explained in the short two-page *Walker* opinion that the Seventh Amendment "as has been many times decided, relates only to trials in the courts of the United States."[15] "The States, so far as this amendment is concerned," he continued, "are left to regulate trials in their own courts in their own way. A trial by jury in suits at common law pending in the State courts is not, therefore, a privilege or immunity of national citizenship."[16] Accordingly, the Fourteenth Amendment did not compel states to provide jury trials for civil matters. States only needed to follow due process of law. As Waite explained, "[a] State cannot deprive a person of his property without due process of law; but this does not necessarily imply that all trials in the State courts affecting the property of persons must be by jury."[17] States were free to determine the conditions under which to use civil jury trials.

Waite suggested that states already followed due process of law, declaring that "[d]ue process of law is process due according to the law of the land. This process in the States is regulated by the law of the State."[18] The Court's responsibility, he continued, "is only to determine whether it is in conflict with the supreme law of the land,—that is to say, with the Constitution and laws of the United States."[19] The due process "requirement of the Constitution is met if the trial is had according to the settled course of judicial proceedings."[20] Court evaluation of a state's administration of due process did not include imposing any specific federal right.

14 *Walker*, 92 U.S. 90, at 92.
15 Ibid.
16 Ibid.
17 Ibid., at 92–93.
18 Ibid., at 93.
19 Ibid.
20 Ibid.

Confirmation

The Court has adhered to the position that the Seventh Amendment civil jury trial guarantee does not extend to the state level and acknowledged *Walker* as the case in which it made this ruling. In decisions addressing the right at the federal level, the Court has not needed to cite *Walker*. For example, in *Galloway v. United States* (1943), a case concerning lower federal courts, Justice Wiley Rutledge elaborated that "the Amendment was designed to preserve the basic institution of jury trial in only its most fundamental elements, not the great mass of procedural forms and details, varying even then so widely among common law jurisdictions."[21] The Court in *Colgrove v. Battin* (1973) followed this perspective to uphold a lower federal court procedure establishing six jurors for civil jury trials.[22] Justice Byron White in *Atlas Roofing v. Occupational Safety Commission* (1977) held that Congress could establish factfinding agencies that did not involve juries, asserting that the Seventh Amendment only preserved the rights that existed at the time of its ratification.[23] In *Tull v. United States* (1987), the Court ruled that the Seventh Amendment did not require that a jury rather than a federal judge impose fines for Clean Water Act violations.[24]

Some justices credit *Walker* along with other cases when explaining that the Court holds that the civil jury right only applies at the federal level. For example, in reference to the Sixth and Seventh Amendments, Justice Benjamin Cardozo in *Palko v. Connecticut* (1937) cited *Walker* and three other decisions in which the Court held that "trial by jury may be modified by a state or abolished altogether."[25] Justices in *Minneapolis & St. Louis Railroad v. Bombolis* (1916), *New York Central Railroad v. White* (1917), and *Wagner Electric v. Lyndon* (1923) also made such ambiguous *Walker* confirmations.[26]

A few justices, however, have recognized *Walker* as the case in which the Court ruled against extending the Seventh Amendment civil jury trial right to the state level. Justice Rufus Peckham in *Maxwell v. Dow* (1900), addressing the necessary number of jurors in state trials, stated that "[i]n *Walker v. Sauvinet*, it was held that a trial by jury in suits at common law in the state courts was not a

21 *Galloway v. United States*, 319 U.S. 372, at 392 (1943).

22 *Colgrove v. Battin*, 413 U.S. 149, at 157 (1973).

23 *Atlas Roofing Co. v. Occupational Safety Commission*, 430 U.S. 442, at 450, 455, 459–60 (1977).

24 *Tull v. United States*, 481 U.S. 412, at 426–27 (1987).

25 *Palko v. Connecticut*, 302 U.S. 319, at 324 (1937).

26 *Minneapolis & St. Louis Railroad Co. v. Bombolis*, 241 U.S. 211, at 217 (1916); *New York Central Railroad Co. v. White*, 243 U.S. 188, at 208 (1917); and *Wagner Electric Co. v. Lyndon*, 262 U.S. 226, at 232 (1923).

privilege or immunity belonging to a person as a citizen of the United States, and protected, therefore, by the Fourteenth Amendment."[27] In *Frank v. Mangum* (1915), Justice Mahlon Pitney, arguing that the Due Process Clause did not impose specific trial rights on states, affirmed that "[t]rial by jury is not essential to it, either in civil cases (*Walker v. Sauvinet*), or in criminal."[28] Justice Hugo Black in his *Adamson v. California* (1947) dissent explained that the Court ruled against making a few Bill of Rights' protections "immune against state invasion," among which he listed "the Seventh Amendment's guarantee of a jury trial in civil cases, *Walker v. Sauvinet*."[29]

While the Court has not recently heard a case regarding the civil jury trial right at the state level, it has ruled on the federal *criminal* jury trial protection. The Court's *Duncan v. Louisiana* (1968) holding that the Due Process Clause incorporated the Sixth Amendment criminal jury trial right did not include the civil jury trial guarantee. White did not mention the Seventh Amendment in *Duncan* and at one point elaborated that not "every criminal trial—or any particular trial—held before a judge alone is unfair or that a defendant may never be as fairly treated by a judge as he would be by a jury."[30] Justice John Harlan II in his dissent cited *Walker* as an example of the Court ignoring the Fourteenth Amendment and following its *Barron* view of the Bill of Rights.[31]

Summary

The civil jury right of the Seventh Amendment could constitutionally apply against states but the Court has denied this possibility. Waite appealed to the Fourteenth Amendment in *Walker*; however, he held that the Seventh Amendment "relates only to trials in the courts of the United States."[32] The Court has not ruled against this position, even though it has since used the Fourteenth Amendment to extend most other Bill of Rights' guarantees to the state level. Some justices have confirmed that the Court in *Walker* held that the civil jury guarantee only protects against the federal government.

27 *Maxwell v. Dow*, 176 U.S. 581, at 594, see also 595 (1900).
28 *Frank v. Mangum*, 237 U.S. 309, at 340 (1915) (citation information omitted).
29 *Adamson v. California*, 332 U.S. 46, at 78 (1947) (Black, H., dissenting).
30 *Duncan v. Louisiana*, 391 U.S. 145, at 158 (1968).
31 Ibid., at 174 n. 9 (Harlan, J., dissenting).
32 *Walker*, 92 U.S. 90, at 92.

Re-examination of Facts

> "In Suits at common law [...] no fact tried by a jury, shall be otherwise re-examined in any Court of the United States, than according to the rules of the common law."

For the Supreme Court, the Seventh Amendment guarantee against re-examining the facts of a civil jury trial only restrains federal courts. This right comes with the caveat that a federal court may re-examine a lower jury trial as long as it follows common law procedures. The Court in *Justices v. Murray* (1870) held that the right to be free from re-examination of civil jury decisions did not apply to the state level.[1]

Before *Justices*

In *Parsons v. Bedford* (1830), Justice Joseph Story asserted that the second clause of the Seventh Amendment "is a prohibition to the courts of the United States to re-examine any facts tried by a jury in any other manner."[2] He explained that

1 *The Justices v. Murray*, 76 U.S. (9 Wall.) 274 (1870).

2 *Parsons v. Bedford*, 28 U.S. (3 Pet.) 433, at 447–48 (1830). This was not Story's first time addressing the Seventh Amendment. In 1812, serving on the circuit, he made similar arguments in *United States v. Wonson*, 28 F. Cas. 745, at 750 (C.C.D. Mass. 1812).

federal courts could re-examine lower court civil jury trial decisions, but they had to follow the "manner" of common law. This meant that

> [t]he only modes known to the common law to re-examine such facts, are the granting of a new trial by the court where the issue was tried, or to which the record was properly returnable; or the award of a venire facias de novo, by an appellate court, for some error of law which intervened in the proceedings.[3]

In the nation's system of justice, federal courts could retry civil jury cases based on "any mistake of the facts."[4] Story elaborated that states used common law before and after the founding.[5] Additionally, Congress's 1789 Judiciary Act provided for suits of law—"the trial of issues in fact"—retrials in all federal courts.[6] While Story described how the Seventh Amendment fit with America's common law retrial process and related to the federal level, he did not address whether either of its two clauses applied to state courts.[7]

In *Lessee of Livingston v. Moore* (1833), Justice William Johnson discussed retrials of civil cases in reference to the federal courts.[8] Johnson adhered to the recent *Barron v. Baltimore* (1833) ruling that Bill of Rights' guarantees only protected against the federal government.[9] He dismissed the plaintiffs' claim that the state violated their Seventh Amendment rights with the blunt explanation that "[a]s to the amendments of the Constitution of the United States, they must be put out of the case, since it is now settled that those amendments do not extend to the states."[10] Johnson elaborated that "[w]hen we find principles distinctly settled by adjudications, and known and acted upon as the law of the land, we have no more right to question them or deviate from them than could be correctly exercised by their own tribunals."[11] Perhaps the Fourteenth Amendment of 1868, which in part protected due process of law from state infringement, would draw into question this *Barron* view of the civil jury retrial prohibition.

3 *Parsons*, 28 U.S. 433, at 448.
4 Ibid., at 449.
5 Ibid., at 446.
6 Ibid., at 447. See *An Act to Establish the Judicial Courts of the United States*, chap. 20, 1 Stat. 73, Sec. 17 (September 24, 1789).
7 For references to *Parsons* as interpreting the Seventh Amendment retrial right as applying only to the federal level, see *Justices*, 76 U.S. 274, at 277; *Railroad Company v. Fraloff*, 100 U.S. 24, at 31–32 (1879); and *Chicago, Burlington & Quincy Railroad Co. v. Chicago*, 166 U.S. 226, at 246 (1897).
8 *Lessee of Livingston v. Moore*, 32 U.S. (7 Pet.) 469 (1833).
9 *Barron ex rel. Tiernan v. City of Baltimore*, 32 U.S. (7 Pet.) 243 (1833).
10 *Livingston*, 32 U.S. 469, at 551–52.
11 Ibid., at 542.

Justices v. Murray (1870)

The Court in *Justices* considered the Bill of Rights' protection against court re-examination of civil jury trials in relation to states. This case addressed a congressional law authorizing federal court retrials of state rulings on writs of error. *Justices* not only dealt with the relationship between federal and state courts, it also occurred after ratification of the Fourteenth Amendment.

Justice Samuel Nelson in the unanimous *Justices* opinion asserted that "the seventh amendment, upon its true construction, applies to a cause tried by a jury in a State court," preventing a federal court from retrying the case outside of common law.[12] This was to say that the prohibition only related to federal courts. The right against courts re-examining civil jury decisions "are confined to those in the Federal courts," he emphasized.[13] Nelson referenced Story's arguments in *Parsons* that each clause stood on its own—with the second forbidding federal courts from re-examining civil trial facts without following common law—and that only the same or an appeals court could retry a civil case and only for factual errors.[14]

The Court now made an important point that was missing in *Parsons*, namely, that "the ten amendments proposed by Congress, and adopted by the States, are limitations upon the powers of the Federal government, and not upon the States," as the Court ruled in *Barron*.[15] Consequently, "the seventh amendment could not be invoked in a State court to prohibit it from re-examining, on a writ of error, facts that had been tried by a jury in the court below."[16] The right against civil jury retrial was federal only; it did not prohibit state courts from re-examining facts from their own lower courts. Nelson did not mention the Fourteenth Amendment or due process of law.

Additionally, state and federal courts followed "the same system of laws," and therefore the Bill of Rights was not needed to enforce common law procedures upon the states.[17] Nelson clarified that because the core of the Seventh Amendment was about "suits at common law, where the trial has been by jury," federal courts could re-examine facts from any court, as long as the issue was federal in nature and the federal retrial followed common law.[18]

12 *Justices*, 76 U.S. 274, at 277.
13 Ibid.
14 Ibid., at 277–78.
15 Ibid., at 278 (citing *Barron*, 32 U.S. 243).
16 *Justices*, 76 U.S. 274, at 278.
17 Ibid., at 279.
18 Ibid.

Confirmation

The Court has confirmed that the Seventh Amendment prohibition against re-examination of civil jury trials does not apply at the state level but has rarely credited *Justices* as the case in which it established this view. For example, in overturning a federal appeals court ruling that had reversed a lower federal civil jury decision, Justice Willis Van Devanter in *Slocum v. New York Life Insurance* (1913) asserted that "the Amendment, which, although not applicable to proceedings in the courts of the several states, is controlling in the federal courts."[19] While he cited some Court rulings concerning the right at the federal level, including *Parsons*, he did not include *Justices*. The Court mentioned *Justices* along with several other cases in *Minneapolis & St. Louis Railroad v. Bombolis* (1916) to support the view that "the Seventh Amendment applies only to proceedings in courts of the United States and does not in any manner whatever govern or regulate trials by jury in state courts."[20]

Justice John Harlan in *Chicago, Burlington & Quincy Railroad v. Chicago* (1897), however, clearly confirmed that the Court in *Justices* interpreted the second clause of the Seventh Amendment as prohibiting federal, not state courts. He cited *Justices* and described that the Court considered whether

> that as by the construction uniformly given to the first clause of the amendment the suits there mentioned were only those in the Federal courts, the words "and no fact tried by a jury," mentioned in the second clause, relate to trial by jury only in such courts.[21]

He elaborated that in *Justices*, the Court held that federal appellate courts could hear cases from any courts, federal or state, as long as they adhered to the Seventh Amendment's common law guarantee. In relation to *Chicago, B & Q*, which concerned a state court ruling, "it would seem to be clear that the last clause of the Seventh Amendment forbids the retrial by this court of the facts tried by the jury in the present case."[22]

The Court has moved away from the *Barron* view that supported its holding in *Justices* that re-examination of civil jury facts only applied to federal courts. Harlan in *Chicago, B & Q* appealed to the Due Process Clause of the Fourteenth Amendment to protect the federal right of just compensation against states. The

19 *Slocum v. New York Life Insurance Co.*, 228 U.S. 364, at 377 (1913).
20 *Minneapolis & St. Louis Railroad Co. v. Bombolis*, 241 U.S. 211, at 217 (1916).
21 *Chicago, B & Q*, 166 U.S. 226, at 243 (citing *Justices*, 76 U.S. 274, at 278).
22 *Chicago, B & Q*, 166 U.S. 226, at 244.

Court in *Twining v. New Jersey* (1908) stepped further away from *Barron* in arguing that the Due Process Clause might extend other Bill of Rights' protections to the state level.[23] Beginning with *Gitlow v. New York* (1925), the Court used to the Due Process Clause to incorporate many federal rights.[24] Nelson's argument in *Justices* that *Barron* prevented the Court from applying the civil jury retrial protection to the states is no longer valid. However, the Court has not returned to the question of whether the Seventh Amendment right against re-examination of civil jury decisions extends to the states.

Summary

The Seventh Amendment prohibition against courts re-examining civil jury trials without following common law procedures is unincorporated. Nelson asserted in *Justices* that retrials of civil jury decisions "are confined to those in the Federal courts."[25] While this sounds like *Parsons*, that case concerned federal courts, whereas *Justices* addressed the Seventh Amendment right at the state level. Along with appealing to the *Barron* view of the Bill of Rights, Nelson presumed that states followed common law practices. Harlan in *Chicago, B & Q* recognized that the Court in *Justices* held that the Seventh Amendment did not limit states from re-examining civil jury decisions.

23 *Twining v. State of New Jersey*, 211 U.S. 78, at 99 (1908).
24 *Gitlow v. People of New York*, 268 U.S. 652, at 666 (1925).
25 *Justices*, 76 U.S. 274, at 277.

PART VIII

EIGHTH AMENDMENT

Excessive Bail

"Excessive bail shall not be required."

The Eighth Amendment concerns the last step in the justice system: government's authority to punish those that courts have found guilty. In its early cases about disproportionate penalties, the Supreme Court did not give attention to the right against excessive bail, instead focusing on the entire amendment. The Court in *Schilb v. Kuebel* (1971) indicated agreement with a lower court ruling and applied the right against excessive bail to the state level.[1]

Before *Schilb*

Initially, the Court ruled that all Eighth Amendment rights related only to the federal government. Referencing *Barron v. Baltimore* (1833), Chief Justice Salmon Chase asserted in *Pervear v. Commonwealth* (1867) that the protection against "excessive, cruel, and unusual" punishment "does not apply to State but to National legislation."[2] The Court affirmed this *Barron* view of the amendment in *O'Neil*

1 *Schilb v. Kuebel*, 404 U.S. 357 (1971).

2 *Pervear v. Commonwealth of Massachusetts*, 72 U.S. (5 Wall.) 475, at 479–80 (1867) (citing *Barron ex rel. Tiernan v. City of Baltimore*, 32 U.S. (7 Pet.) 243 (1833)).

v. Vermont (1892) with Justice Samuel Blatchford asserting that "it has always been ruled that the 8th Amendment to the Constitution of the United States does not apply to the States" and referencing *Pervear* for support.[3]

However, Justice Stephen Field and Justice John Harlan in their *O'Neil* dissents each argued that the Fourteenth Amendment protected the entire Eighth Amendment at the state level. Field described that "[t]he whole inhibition is against that which is excessive either in the bail required, or fine imposed, or punishment inflicted."[4] Furthermore, he contended that the Bill of Rights restricted government "and the Fourteenth Amendment, as to all such rights, places a limit upon state power by ordaining that no State shall make or enforce any law which shall abridge them."[5] For Harlan in his *O'Neil* dissent, the Fourteenth Amendment protected from state infringement "the fundamental rights of life, liberty or property," among which he included the guarantees of the Eighth Amendment.[6]

Years later, after the Court incorporated some other federal rights, the Eighth Circuit Federal Appeals Court in *Pilkinton v. Circuit Court of Howell County* (8th Cir. 1963) asserted that the right prohibiting excessive bail was incorporated. The court in its two-page *per curiam* opinion stated simply that "[w]e take it for granted that [...] the prohibition in the Eighth Amendment against requiring excessive bail must now be regarded as applying to the States, under the Fourteenth Amendment."[7] It did not mention due process specifically. Lower federal court decisions, however, are not binding throughout the nation, although the Court could find them persuasive.

Schilb v. Kuebel (1971)

The Court in its 4-3 *Schilb* opinion assumed that the right against excessive bail existed at the state level. This case addressed the issue of Illinois keeping 1% of a person's bail bond as an administration fee, even if a court found the accused innocent.

The concept of fundamental rights related to the protection of excessive bail against states. Justice Harry Blackmun explained that "[b]ail, of course, is basic to our system of law, and the Eighth Amendment's proscription of excessive

3 *O'Neil v. Vermont*, 144 U.S. 323, at 332 (1892) (citing *Pervear*, 72 U.S. 475).
4 *O'Neil*, 144 U.S. 323, at 340 (Field, S., dissenting).
5 Ibid., at 363.
6 Ibid., at 370 (Harlan, J., dissenting).
7 *Pilkinton v. Circuit Court of Howell County, Missouri*, 324 F.2d 45, at 46 (8th Cir. 1963) (citation information omitted).

bail has been assumed to have application to the States through the Fourteenth Amendment."[8] This was the Court's first affirmative statement about the incorporation status of the excessive bail prohibition. Blackmun did not mention the Due Process Clause; however, he referenced *Pilkinton* and *Robinson v. California* (1962) to support this claim. As mentioned, a lower federal court in *Pilkinton* regarded the right of no excessive bail incorporated, appealing to the Fourteenth Amendment. In *Robinson*, Douglas argued that the right against cruel and unusual punishment "is applicable to the States by reason of the Due Process Clause of the Fourteenth Amendment."[9]

Blackmun clarified, however, that "we are not at all concerned here with any fundamental right to bail or with any Eighth Amendment-Fourteenth Amendment question of bail excessiveness" because the issue was just a small administration fee.[10] He ruled that the state collection of a fee from those released on bail bonds did not violate equal protection or fundamental rights.[11] Blackmun reasoned that the state had a "rational basis" for retaining a minor fee, which was to help offset the burden that bail procedures placed on administration.[12]

Confirmation

The Court has recognized that it has incorporated freedom from excessive bail and did so in *Schilb*. Occasionally, a justice neglects to mention *Schilb* when explaining that the guarantee restricts state governments. For example, Justice William Brennan in *Furman v. Georgia* (1972) regarded the prohibition on disproportionate bail as extending to the state level yet cited no incorporation case.[13] Such missing references are expected, however, since the Court in *Schilb* assumed rather than ruled that the federal right limited states.

However, more than one justice has identified *Schilb* as the incorporation case for the right against excessive bail. Justice William Rehnquist in *Baker v. McCollan* (1979) stated that "[w]e of course agree with the dissent's quotation of the statement from *Schilb v. Kuebel* (1971), that 'the Eighth Amendment's proscription of excessive bail has been assumed to have application to the States through

8 Ibid., at 365 (citation information omitted).
9 *Robinson v. California*, 370 U.S. 660, at 675 (1962) (Douglas, W., concurring).
10 *Schilb*, 404 U.S. 357, at 365.
11 Ibid., at 357, 365.
12 Ibid., at 367.
13 *Furman v. Georgia*, 408 U.S. 238, at 279–80 (1972) (Brennan, W., concurring).

the Fourteenth Amendment.'"[14] In the excessive fines case of *Browning-Ferris Industries v. Kelco Disposal* (1989), Justice Sandra Day O'Connor stated that "the Court has assumed that the Excessive Bail Clause of the Eighth Amendment applies to the States. See *Schilb v. Kuebel* (1971)."[15] Justice Samuel Alito in his *McDonald v. Chicago* (2010) listing of incorporated rights gave a more definitive statement, writing simply, "[w]ith respect to the Eighth Amendment, see [...] *Schilb v. Kuebel* (1971) (prohibition against excessive bail)."[16]

Summary

Schilb provides the Court's statement on the incorporation status of the right to be free from excessive bail. For Blackmun, "the Eighth Amendment's proscription of excessive bail has been assumed to have application to the States through the Fourteenth Amendment."[17] Subsequently, a few justices have confirmed that the Court in *Schilb* assumed that this federal protection extended to the state level.

14 *Baker v. McCollan*, 443 U.S. 137, at 144 n. 3; see also 149 n. 1 (Stevens, J., dissenting) (1979) (citation information omitted).

15 *Browning-Ferris Industries of Vermont, Inc. v. Kelco Disposal, Inc.*, 492 U.S. 257, at 284 (1989) (O'Connor, S., partial dissenting; citation information omitted).

16 *McDonald v. City of Chicago*, 561 U.S. 742, at 764 n. 12 (2010).

17 *Schilb*, 404 U.S. 357, at 365.

Excessive Fines

"[N]or excessive fines imposed."

The Eighth Amendment protection against excessive fines is the most recently incorporated right. The Supreme Court ruled in *Timbs v. Indiana* (2019) that the guarantee applied to the state level because it was fundamental to the American system of justice.[1] Before then, justices recognized that the Court had not yet incorporated the right.[2]

Before *Timbs*

The Court refused to extend any Eighth Amendment rights to the states in *Pervear v. Commonwealth* (1867) and *O'Neil v. Vermont* (1892) by appealing to the *Barron v. Baltimore* (1833) view that the Bill of Rights did not protect against state

1 *Timbs v. Indiana*, 586 U.S. ___ (2019).

2 See, for example, *United States v. Bajakajian*, 524 U.S. 321, at 327 (1998); and *McDonald v. City of Chicago*, 561 U.S. 742, at 765 n. 13 (2010).

governments.[3] However, Chief Justice Salmon Chase in *Pervear* indicated that the Court might take into consideration the excessiveness of fines. In this case, the state punished the defendant for keeping and selling alcohol with a $50 fine and three months of hard labor imprisonment. Chase reasoned that even if the Eighth Amendment limited state governments, the Court would still not rule against the state in this case because this punishment was not "excessive or cruel or unusual."[4]

In *Browning-Ferris Industries v. Kelco Disposal* (1989), the Court rejected consideration of incorporating the right against excessive fines.[5] Justice Harry Blackmun in *Browning-Ferris* supported the idea of the Eighth Amendment prohibiting any government in the United States from imposing excessive fines, bail, and punishment.[6] However, the Court was declining to specifically rule on whether the immunity from excessive fines protected individuals against states because the petitioners had not raised the issue.[7]

While Justice Sandra Day O'Connor concurred with the *Browning-Ferris* ruling that the appellant did not present a due process claim, she dissented from the Court's refusal to incorporate the excessive fines protections. She noted that the Court in *Francis v. Resweber* (1947) presumed that the Eighth Amendment prohibition against cruel and unusual punishment applied at the state level and decidedly incorporated it in *Robinson v. California* (1962).[8] O'Connor in *Browning-Ferris* explained that the Court recently assumed incorporation of the right against excessive bail in *Schilb v. Kuebel* (1971).[9] Therefore, she asserted, "I see no reason to distinguish one Clause of the Eighth Amendment from another for purposes of incorporation, and would hold that the Excessive Fines Clause also applies to the States."[10]

3 *Pervear v. Commonwealth of Massachusetts*, 72 U.S. (5 Wall.) 475, at 480 (1867) (citing *Barron ex rel. Tiernan v. City of Baltimore*, 32 U.S. (7 Pet.) 243 (1833)); and *O'Neil v. Vermont*, 144 U.S. 323, at 332 (1892) (citing *Pervear*, 72 U.S. 475).

4 *Pervear*, 72 U.S. 475, at 480.

5 *Browning-Ferris Industries of Vermont, Inc. v. Kelco Disposal, Inc.*, 492 U.S. 257 (1989).

6 Ibid., at 275.

7 Ibid., at 276–77.

8 Ibid., at 284 (O'Connor, S., partial dissenting; citing *Louisiana ex rel. Francis v. Resweber*, 329 U.S. 459 (1947); and *Robinson v. California*, 370 U.S. 660 (1962)).

9 *Browning-Ferris*, 492 U.S. 257, at 284 (O'Connor, S., partial dissenting; citing *Schilb v. Kuebel*, 404 U.S. 357, at 365 (1971)).

10 *Browning-Ferris*, 492 U.S. 257, at 284 (O'Connor, S., partial dissenting).

Timbs v. Indiana (2019)

In *Timbs*, the Court with a 9-0 vote held that the federal right against excessive fines applied at the state level. This case concerned the state trying to keep the guilty party's vehicle that was valued at four times the $10,000 maximum allowable fine for a drug-dealing conviction.

Justice Ruth Bader Ginsburg in the *Timbs* opinion appealed to familiar language to defend incorporating the right of no excessive fines into the Due Process Clause. Using passages from *McDonald v. Chicago* (2010), she asserted that the protection against excessive fines "is 'fundamental to our scheme of ordered liberty,' with 'dee[p] root[s] in [our] history and tradition.'"[11] She reiterated this reasoning throughout the opinion. For example, she elaborated that "[a] Bill of Rights protection is incorporated, we have explained, if it is 'fundamental to our scheme of ordered liberty,' or 'deeply rooted in this Nation's history and tradition.'"[12] Ginsburg did not mention that the Court initially developed this incorporation approach in *Snyder v. Massachusetts* (1934) and *Palko v. Connecticut* (1937).[13] Regardless, "[t]he Excessive Fines Clause is therefore incorporated by the Due Process Clause of the Fourteenth Amendment," she ruled.[14]

Ginsburg also followed the *Malloy v. Hogan* (1964) standard that "[i]ncorporated Bill of Rights guarantees are 'enforced against the States under the Fourteenth Amendment according to the same standards that protect those personal rights against federal encroachment.'"[15] She explained that this "same standards" requirement meant that "if a Bill of Rights protection is incorporated, there is no daylight between the federal and state conduct it prohibits or requires."[16]

Referencing *Browning-Ferris*, Ginsburg argued that all Eighth Amendment rights limit the abuse of power because, "[t]aken together, these Clauses place 'parallel limitations' on 'the power of those entrusted with the criminal-law function of government.'"[17] She explained that "[e]xorbitant tolls undermine other constitutional liberties. Excessive fines can be used, for example, to retaliate against or

11 *Timbs*, 586 U.S.___, at 2 (bracketed additions in original; quoting *McDonald*, 561 U.S. 742, at 767).
12 *Timbs*, 586 U.S.___, at 3 (citing *McDonald*, 561 U.S. 742, at 767).
13 See *Snyder v. Massachusetts*, 291 U.S. 97, at 105 (1934); and *Palko v. Connecticut*, 302 U.S. 319, at 325, 326 (1937).
14 *Timbs*, 586 U.S.___, at 2.
15 *Timbs*, 586 U.S.___, at 3 (citing *McDonald*, 561 U.S. 742, at 767, quoting *Malloy v. Hogan*, 378 U.S. 1, at 10 (1964)).
16 *Timbs*, 586 U.S.___, at 3.
17 Ibid. (citing *Browning-Ferris*, 492 U.S. 257, at 263, quoting *Ingraham v. Wright*, 430 U.S. 651, at 664 (1977)).

chill the speech of political enemies."[18] Protection against excessive fines is a fundamental right and "[t]oday, acknowledgement of the right's fundamental nature remains widespread."[19] However, the precise defense was not as important as the Court's interpretation that a federal right was incorporated. As Ginsburg added near the end of the opinion, "regardless of whether application of the Excessive Fines Clause to civil *in rem* forfeitures is itself fundamental or deeply rooted, our conclusion that the Clause is incorporated remains unchanged."[20]

Confirmation

The Court has acknowledged that it extended the right against excessive fines to the state level and recognized *Timbs* as the incorporation case. Some justices have mentioned *Timbs* in recent discussions about incorporation but not its protection of the excessive fines prohibition. For example, Justice Clarence Thomas referenced *Timbs* when discussing Court's use of the Due Process Clause for incorporating federal rights in *Gamble v. United States* (2019).[21] In *Ramos v. Louisiana* (2020), Justice Neil Gorsuch cited *Timbs* as a recent example of the Court's consensus that incorporated rights follow the same standards of protection at both federal and state levels.[22] However, Justice Samuel Alito in his *Ramos* dissent clearly stated that among the "provisions of the Bill of Rights [that] apply with full force to the States, see *Timbs* (Eighth Amendment's Excessive Fines Clause)."[23]

Summary

The Court has incorporated the Eighth Amendment protection against government imposing excessive fines. It made this ruling in *Timbs*, with Ginsburg conclusively stating at the end of the opinion that "regardless of whether application of the Excessive Fines Clause to civil *in rem* forfeitures is itself fundamental or deeply rooted, our conclusion that the Clause is incorporated remains unchanged."[24] The following year, Alito confirmed this most recent development in the Court's long line of incorporated rights.

18 *Timbs*, 586 U.S. ___, at 6.
19 Ibid.
20 Ibid., at 9 (emphasis in original).
21 *Gamble v. United States*, 587 U.S. ___, at 17 (2019) (Thomas, C., concurring).
22 *Ramos v. Louisiana*, 590 U.S. ___, at 9 n. 32, see also 10 n. 34, 21 n. 63 (2020).
23 Ibid., at 19 (Alito, S., dissenting; citation information omitted).
24 *Timbs*, 586 U.S. ___, at 2.

Cruel and Unusual Punishments

"[N]or cruel and unusual punishments inflicted."

In addressing "cruel and unusual punishments" over the years, the Supreme Court refined the meaning of such punishments and ruled in favor of state discretion over punishing the guilty. Later, in *Robinson v. California* (1962), it incorporated the right against cruel and unusual punishments.[1]

Before *Robinson*

The Court rejected using any Eighth Amendment guarantees to protect against state punishments in *Pervear v. Commonwealth* (1867) and *O'Neil v. Vermont* (1892).[2] In these opinions, it relied on the *Barron v. Baltimore* (1833) holding that the Bill of Rights only related to the federal government. However, while Chief Justice Salmon Chase in *Pervear* explained that the Eighth Amendment "does not apply to state, but to national, legislation," he added that even if it did protect

1 *Robinson v. California*, 370 U.S. 660 (1962).

2 *Pervear v. Commonwealth of Massachusetts*, 72 U.S. (5 Wall.) 475, at 480 n. 3 (1867); and *O'Neil v. Vermont*, 144 U.S. 323, at 332 (1892). See *Barron ex rel. Tiernan v. City of Baltimore*, 32 U.S. (7 Pet.) 243 (1833).

against states, a $50 fine and three months of hard labor was not "excessive or cruel or unusual."[3]

In *Wilkerson v. Utah* (1879), the Court held that the Eighth Amendment prohibition on cruel and unusual punishments did not cover execution by public shooting, as this punishment was not a form of torture.[4] Justice Nathan Clifford in *Wilkerson*, however, argued that a society having a "Constitution and laws" should avoid "unnecessary cruelty."[5] In the case of *In re Kemmler* (1890), the Court added "lingering death" to the definition of cruel and unusual punishments and did not incorporate the right, arguing that the Fourteenth Amendment did nothing more than assert that national and state governments both used due process of law.[6]

In *O'Neil*, a case about a sentence of just over $6,600 in fines and taxes along with 54 years of hard labor for selling some alcohol, the Court affirmed that Eighth Amendment protections did not extend to the state level.[7] Referring to *Pervear*, Justice Samuel Blatchford stated plainly that "it has always been ruled that the Eighth Amendment to the Constitution of the United States does not apply to the States."[8]

However, the dissenting justices in *O'Neil* conveyed the opposite view about the Eighth Amendment, in particular its prohibition on cruel and unusual punishments. Justice Stephen Field argued that the Fourteenth Amendment "places a limit upon state power by ordaining that no State shall make or enforce any law which shall abridge" Bill of Rights' protections, including "punishments which are cruel and unusual."[9] Along with arguing that the entire Bill of Rights applied at the state level, Field regarded the punishment of 54 years of hard labor as "greatly beyond anything required by any humane law for the offenses."[10] In his *O'Neil* dissent, Justice John Harlan agreed with Field, adding that the Fourteenth Amendment protected fundamental rights, including those of the Eighth Amendment. As he explained, "since the adoption of the Fourteenth Amendment, no one of the fundamental rights of life, liberty, or property, recognized and guaranteed by the Constitution of the United States, can be denied or abridged by a State," which he elaborated included "immunity from cruel and unusual punishments secured by the Eighth Amendment against Federal action, and by the Fourteenth Amendment against

3 *Pervear*, 72 U.S. 475, at 480.
4 *Wilkerson v. Utah*, 99 U.S. 130, at 134–36 (1879).
5 Ibid., at 136.
6 *In re Kemmler*, 136 U.S. 436, at 447–49 (1890).
7 *O'Neil*, 144 U.S. 323, at 332.
8 Ibid.
9 Ibid., at 363 (Field, S., dissenting).
10 Ibid., at 340.

denial or abridgment by the States."[11] Harlan too felt that the hard labor sentence in this case "inflicts punishment, which, in view of the character of the offenses committed, must be deemed cruel and unusual."[12]

The Court in its 5-4 *Francis v. Resweber* (1947) decision regarded the "infliction of unnecessary pain" as cruel and unusual and therefore, Justice Stanley Reed asserted, "[t]he Fourteenth would prohibit by its due process clause execution by a state in a cruel manner."[13] This case involved a planned second electrocution in the chair following a failed first attempt. The Court ruled that going through the process of a second electrocution did not violate the Bill of Rights' protection against cruel and unusual punishment because it was not a deliberate effort to inflict suffering. After all, Reed surmised, "accidents happen."[14] While the Fourteenth Amendment could extend the right against cruel and unusual punishments to the states, it protected only against an intentionally cruel "method," not a mistake.[15]

Robinson v. California (1962)

The Court ruled 6-2 in *Robinson* that the Eighth Amendment guarantee to be free from cruel and unusual punishments applied to the state level. The case concerned a state law allowing punishment for narcotic addiction. Justice Potter Stewart argued that 90 days in prison was a cruel and unusual response to addiction, which California and the Court agreed was a medical illness.[16] Citing *Francis* for support, Stewart elaborated that "a law which made a criminal offense of such a disease would doubtless be universally thought to be an infliction of cruel and unusual punishment in violation of the Eighth and Fourteenth Amendments."[17] He did not specifically mention the Due Process Clause. With this ruling, however, the Court applied the right against cruel and unusual punishments through the Fourteenth Amendment to the state level.

Justice William Douglas in his concurring opinion agreed, emphasizing that "[t]he command of the Eighth Amendment, banning 'cruel and unusual punishments,' [...] is applicable to the States by reason of the Due Process Clause

11 Ibid., at 370 (Harlan, J., dissenting).
12 Ibid., at 371.
13 *Louisiana ex rel. Francis v. Resweber*, 329 U.S. 459, at 463 (1947).
14 Ibid., at 462.
15 Ibid., at 464.
16 *Robinson*, 370 U.S. 660, at 667.
17 Ibid., at 666 (citing *Francis*, 329 U.S. 459).

of the Fourteenth Amendment."[18] Citing *O'Neil*, he argued that "[a] punishment out of all proportion to the offense may bring it within the ban against 'cruel and unusual punishments.'"[19]

Confirmation

The Court has confirmed that *Robinson* is the incorporation case for the right against cruel and unusual punishment. It is uncommon for a justice not to connect *Robinson* with this right when discussing the decision in relation to incorporation. One exception is Justice Arthur Goldberg in *Griswold v. Connecticut* (1965) who listed several incorporation cases in a note, including *Robinson*, but did not mention which right each case protected.[20]

Some justices have been clear as to which case the Court incorporated the right of no cruel and unusual punishments. Returning to Goldberg, he stated in his concurring opinion of *Pointer v. Texas* (1965) that "the Court has held that the Fourteenth Amendment guarantees against infringement by the States [...] the Eighth Amendment's prohibition of cruel and unusual punishments" and referenced *Robinson* as the incorporation case.[21] Justice William Brennan in *Malloy v. Hogan* (1964) and *Furman v. Georgia* (1972) explained that the Court in *Robinson* used the Due Process Clause to extend the Bill of Rights' protection to the states.[22] So too did Justice Hugo Black in *Gideon v. Wainwright* (1963) and Justice Sandra Day O'Connor in *Browning-Ferris Industries v. Kelco Disposal* (1989).[23] In his extensive list of incorporated rights in *McDonald v. Chicago* (2010), Justice Samuel Alito stated, "[w]ith respect to the Eighth Amendment, see *Robinson v. California* (1962) (cruel and unusual punishment)"[24]

18 *Robinson*, 370 U.S. 660, at 675 (Douglas, W., concurring).

19 Ibid., at 676 (Douglas, W., concurring; citing *O'Neil*, 144 U.S. 323, at 331).

20 *Griswold v. Connecticut*, 381 U.S. 479, at 488 n. 2 (1965) (Goldberg, A., concurring).

21 *Pointer v. Texas*, 380 U.S. 400, at 411–12 n. 6 (1965).

22 *Malloy v. Hogan*, 378 U.S. 1, at 6 n. 6 (1964); and *Furman v. Georgia*, 408 U.S. 238, at 257 n. 1 (1972) (Brennan, W., concurring).

23 *Gideon v. Wainwright*, 372 U.S. 335, at 341–42 n. 7 (1963); and *Browning-Ferris Industries of Vermont, Inc. v. Kelco Disposal, Inc.*, 492 U.S. 257, at 284 (1989) (O'Connor, S., partial dissenting).

24 *McDonald v. City of Chicago*, 561 U.S. 742, at 764–65 n. 12 (2010) (citation information omitted).

Summary

The Court in *Robinson* explicitly incorporated the right against cruel and unusual punishments. As Douglas asserted, the right "is applicable to the States."[25] Justices have since acknowledged that the Court applied the right to the state level in *Robinson*.

25 *Robinson*, 370 U.S. 660, at 675.

Conclusion

This review of the Supreme Court's incorporation of the Bill of Rights has identified 23 out of 29 enumerated federal rights that the Court has extended to the state level. As Justice Ruth Bader Ginsburg explained in the most recent incorporation case of *Timbs v. Indiana* (2019), "[w]ith only 'a handful' of exceptions, this Court has held that the Fourteenth Amendment's Due Process Clause incorporates the protections contained in the Bill of Rights, rendering them applicable to the States."[1] This analysis has also revealed that the Court has not given some incorporation cases much attention.

Unincorporated Rights

The Court has not incorporated some rights for various reasons. It has not heard cases on the issue for two guarantees. It ruled long ago against extending one federal protection to the state level. It has not incorporated a few rights because it considers states as already protecting them. As Table 1 displays, six federal rights remain unincorporated.

1 *Timbs v. Indiana*, 586 U.S. ___, at 2–3 (2019) (citing *McDonald v. City of Chicago*, 561 U.S. 742, at 764–65 n. 12–13 (2010)).

Table 1: Unincorporated Rights

Third Amendment	**Sixth Amendment**
No Quartering of Soldiers	Jury Trial in State and District of Crime
Fifth Amendment	**Seventh Amendment**
Grand Jury Indictment	Civil Jury Trial
Due Process of Law	No Re-Examination of Facts

One of the few federal rights that the Court has simply never considered for incorporation is the Third Amendment protection against government housing of soldiers in private homes during peacetime. Lower federal courts have assumed that this prohibition on the federal government also guards against state governments. The Court seems receptive to rule the same but has not had the opportunity to either agree or disagree with the lower court holding that the right of no quartering of soldiers exists at the state level.

The Court in *Hurtado v. California* (1884) ruled against extending to the state level the Fifth Amendment right of grand jury indictments for capital offenses.[2] In that decision, Justice Stanley Matthews argued that states already followed due process of law, the details of which rested on the will of the people within each state. While the grand jury hearing was a specific feature of the federal criminal justice system, the Court held that states were free to implement their own procedures of justice, such as using preliminary information rather than grand jury hearings. The Court has since stood by this decision.

The Court has not incorporated the Fifth Amendment right of due process of law. It presumes that all states already use due process—it is the "law of the land." It also sees the Fourteenth Amendment as providing additional support with the guarantee that the federal government will protect due process of law at the state level. Initially, a lower federal court in 1880 used the Due Process Clause of the Fourteenth Amendment to overturn a state law. The Court in *Scott v. McNeal* (1894) unanimously agreed that the Due Process Clause applied to the state level, thereby establishing that the Fifth Amendment due process right remained a federal protection.[3] It has used the Fifth Amendment provision to overturn federal, not state, laws. The Court simply does not regard the Fifth Amendment due process right as germane for incorporation.

As with the Third Amendment, the Court has not considered for incorporation the Sixth Amendment guarantee of a criminal trial jury comprised of

2 *Hurtado v. People of California*, 110 U.S. 516 (1884).

3 *Scott v. McNeal*, 154 U.S. 34 (1894).

members from the same state and district in which the crime occurred. Yet, also like the Third Amendment, a lower appeals court ruled in favor of incorporating the right. A federal appeals court assumed in *Zicarelli v. Gray* (3d Cir. 1976) that the vicinage protection requires a state to draw jurors only from a federal district in which the crime took place.[4] The Court seems to regard the civil jury composition right as part and parcel of national and state criminal justice systems, sometimes mentioning it when quoting passages from the Sixth Amendment. However, it has not heard a case regarding the application of this right to the states.

The Court has not incorporated the two Seventh Amendment rights of providing for civil jury trials and prohibiting courts from re-examining facts of civil jury trials without following common law procedures. Overall, it held that these rights do not need to be incorporated because states already use common law, negating a reason for extending them to the states. In *Walker v. Sauvinet* (1876), the Court ruled that the civil trial protection only applied to federal courts, and that states were free to determine specific trial procedures as long as they followed due process of law.[5] In the earlier case of *Justices v. Murray* (1870), it simply followed the *Barron v. Baltimore* (1833) perspective that the Bill of Rights did not apply at the state level to rule that the civil jury retrial protection was federal only.[6] The Court has since repudiated the *Barron* view; however, it has not recently heard cases addressing incorporation of these rights.

Regardless of the reasons for not incorporating a few Bill of Rights' guarantees, the Court could extend any of them to the states. This may be especially true for the two unincorporated rights that lower federal courts assume restrict state governments: no housing of soldiers in private homes without consent and juries drawn from the same state and district as the related crimes. It might also be relatively simple for the Court to incorporate the two Seventh Amendment civil jury protections since their current unincorporated status rests in part on the dated *Barron* view of the Bill of Rights. The Court would probably need to explain that application of the Fifth Amendment right of due process to the states was nothing more than a restatement or recognition of the same general "law of the land" protection of the Fourteenth Amendment. Incorporating the grand jury requirement would require several states to implement some new criminal justice procedures.

4 *Zicarelli v. Gray*, 543 F.2d 466, at 479 (3d Cir. 1976).

5 *Walker v. Sauvinet*, 92 U.S. 90, at 92–3 (1876).

6 *The Justices v. Murray*, 76 U.S. (9 Wall.) 274, at 278 (1870) (citing *Barron ex rel. Tiernan v. City of Baltimore*, 32 U.S. (7 Pet.) 243 (1833)).

Incorporated Rights

The Court has incorporated most of the first eight amendments (see Table 2). The first right that the Court incorporated was just compensation in 1897. Later, it embraced the rationale that the Fourteenth Amendment due process of law protection of liberty included "fundamental rights," and incorporated speech in 1925, press in 1931, assembly in 1937, and the two religion protections in 1940 and 1947. Some justices in the 1940s held that the entire First Amendment applied to the state level.[7] However, the Court did not complete incorporation of all First Amendment rights until 1963 with the right to petition government. The Court had a heightened period of incorporation from 1962 to 1971, when it applied 12 rights to the states, most from the Fifth and Sixth Amendments. It did not incorporate another Bill of Rights' guarantee until 2010, with keep and bear firearms and again in 2019 with no excessive fines. Appendix C lists the Court's establishment of each right's incorporation status in chronological order.

Others have probed possible reasons for the ebb and flow of incorporation.[8] Suffice to say that, as insulated as the founders tried to make the Court from the influence of factional interests, it is not isolated from politics. For example, Democratic presidents appointed every member of Chief Justice Fred Vinson's Court of 1946–1949—a Court that extended four Bill of Rights' guarantees to the state level in that short time. When the Court incorporated 11 rights, 1962–1969, it always had five Democratic-appointed members, not including Republican nominee Chief Justice Earl Warren.

In its most recent incorporation cases, the Court altered the theoretical due process defense for extending federal rights to the state level. Justice Hugo Black in *Gideon v. Wainwright* (1963) captured the Court's prevailing incorporation theory around that time when he explained that "those guarantees of the Bill of Rights which are fundamental safeguards of liberty immune from federal abridgment

7 *Cantwell v. Connecticut*, 310 U.S. 296, at 303 (1940); and *Everson v. Board of Education of the Township of Ewing*, 330 U.S. 1, at 13, at 15 (1947).

8 See, for example, Richard C. Cortner, *The Supreme Court and the Second Bill of Rights: The Fourteenth Amendment and the Nationalization of Civil Liberties* (Madison: University of Wisconsin Press, 1981); Howard Gillman, "Preferred Freedoms: The Progressive Expansion of State Power and the Rise of Modern Civil Liberties Jurisprudence," *Political Research Quarterly* 47, no. 3 (September 1994), 623–53; Richard A. Primus, *The American Language of Rights* (New York: Cambridge University Press, 1999); Lucas A. Powe Jr., *The Warren Court and American Politics* (Cambridge, MA: Harvard University Press, 2002); and Victoria F. Nourse, "A Tale of Two Lochners: The Untold History of Substantive Due Process and the Idea of Fundamental Rights," *California Law Review* 97, no. 3 (June 2009), 751–99.

Table 2: Incorporated Rights

First Amendment	**Sixth Amendment**
Religion (Establishment)	Speedy Trial
Religion (Free Exercise)	Public Trial
Freedom of Speech	Jury Trial
Freedom of the Press	Impartial Jury
Peaceful Assembly	Informed of Accusation
Petition for Redress of Grievances	Confrontation of Witness
Second Amendment	Defense Witness
Keep and Bear Arms	Counsel
Fourth Amendment	**Eighth Amendment**
No Unreasonable Search and Seizure	No Excessive Bail
Warrant Requirement	No Excessive Fines
Fifth Amendment	No Cruel and Unusual Punishment
No Double Jeopardy	
No Self-Incrimination	
Just Compensation	

are equally protected against state invasion by the Due Process Clause of the Fourteenth Amendment."[9] In *Duncan v. Louisiana* (1968) and *Benton v. Maryland* (1969), however, the Court incorporated rights that were "fundamental to the American scheme of justice."[10] Later, in *McDonald v. Chicago* (2010) and *Timbs*, Justice Samuel Alito and Ginsburg respectively defended incorporation of rights that were "fundamental to our scheme of ordered liberty."[11] Ginsburg added that the exact theoretical defense did not matter as much as the Court's decision to incorporate a right.

The Court has been somewhat unconvincing about the incorporation of a few rights. These are instances in which it did not clearly state something along the lines of "we rule that this specific right is incorporated into the Due Process Clause of the Fourteenth Amendment and therefore now applies at the state level." For example, it is not immediately apparent that the Court in *Gitlow v. New York* (1925), *Near v. Minnesota* (1931), and *De Jonge v. Oregon* (1937) respectively incorporated speech, press, and assembly because these opinions also addressed other

9 *Gideon v. Wainwright*, 372 U.S. 335, at 341.

10 *Duncan v. Louisiana*, 391 U.S. 145, at 149 (1968); and *Benton v. Maryland*, 395 U.S. 784, at 795 (1969).

11 *McDonald*, 561 U.S. 742, at 767; and *Timbs*, 586 U.S. ___, at 2, 3.

First Amendment rights.[12] Moreover, the Court in *Gitlow* merely "assumed" that the federal right applied to the state level. It did the same in *Schilb v. Kuebel* (1971) for no excessive bail.[13]

In a few incorporation cases, the Court did not specifically appeal to the Due Process Clause, including *Everson v. Board of Education* (1947) for freedom against government establishment of religion, *Edwards v. South Carolina* (1963) for the right to petition government, and *Klopfer*.[14] In *Aguilar v. Texas* (1964), the Court incorporated the right of a valid search warrant but cited an earlier case for its reasoning.[15] These opinions defended state application of federal rights with the Fourteenth Amendment and previous cases in which justices appealed to the Due Process Clause. Nevertheless, the Court in each case provided a statement about the federal right's incorporation standing. However thin these defenses may have been, the Court extended Bill of Rights' guarantees to the states in these decisions, which one or more justices have since confirmed.

Confirmation of Incorporated Rights

The Court has confirmed nearly all incorporated rights, some more than others. A precise count of affirming references is not possible due to the sometimes ambiguous discussions surrounding incorporated rights. Yet, as this analysis demonstrates, justices often made clear and succinct statements that the Court applied a federal civil liberty to the state level and did so in a certain case. The one exception appears to be *Parker v. Gladden* (1966), in which the Court protected the right to an impartial jury against state infringement.[16] Justices have acknowledged that the right holds force at the state level but have not clearly recognized *Parker* as the incorporation case. As this review did not investigate every Court decision, further research may find additional incorporation statements. However, within the parameters used to determine cases to analyze, the "Clear Confirmations" column in Tables 3 and 4 offers a comparative account. The average number Court acknowledgments is six for the 23 incorporation cases.

12 *Gitlow v. People of New York*, 268 U.S. 652 (1925); *Near v. State of Minnesota ex rel. Olson*, 283 U.S. 697 (1931); and *De Jonge v. Oregon*, 299 U.S. 353 (1937).

13 *Schilb v. Kuebel*, 404 U.S. 357, at 365 (1971).

14 *Everson*, 330 U.S. 1, at 15 (1947); *Edwards v. South Carolina*, 372 U.S. 229, at 235 (1963); and *Klopfer v. North Carolina*, 386 U.S. 213, at 223 (1967).

15 *Aguilar v. Texas*, 378 U.S. 108, at 110 (1964).

16 *Parker v. Gladden*, 385 U.S. 363 (1966).

Table 3: Six or Fewer Confirmations

Amendment, Right	Relevant Incorporation Case	Clear Confirmations
Sixth, Impartial Jury	*Parker v. Gladden* (1966)	0
Fourth, Valid Search Warrant	*Aguilar v. Texas* (1964)	1
Eighth, No Excessive Fines	*Timbs v. Indiana* (2019)	1
First, Petition Government	*Edwards v. South Carolina* (1963)	2
First, Freedom of Speech	*Gitlow v. New York* (1925)	3
First, Freedom of the Press	*Near v. Minnesota* (1931)	3
First, Peaceably Assemble	*De Jonge v. Oregon* (1937)	3
Eighth, No Excessive Bail	*Schilb v. Kuebel* (1971)	3
Sixth, Informed of Accusation	*Cole v. Arkansas* (1948)	4
Second, Keep and Bear Arms	*McDonald v. Chicago* (2010)	4
First, Religious Exercise	*Cantwell v. Connecticut* (1940)	5
First, No Religious Establishment	*Everson v. Board of Education* (1947)	6
Eighth, No Cruel and Unusual Punishment	*Robinson v. California* (1962)	6

Table 3 lists cases with six or fewer Court confirmations. While *McDonald* and *Timbs* are too recent to have many confirmations, other incorporation cases that justices have rarely recognized may indicate vaguely incorporated rights, at least from the Court's perspective.

Multiple acknowledgments (above the average) of a case in which the Court applied a federal protection to the state level may reflect a favorite right among justices. Table 4 identifies these rights according to the Court's number of confirmations.

The Court tends to extend respect to unanimous rulings, such as *Gideon*, *Pointer*, *Klopfer*, and *Washington*. There are exceptions to this generalization, of course, like *De Jonge*, *Cantwell*, and *Cole*, each of which the Court has only clearly cited a handful of times for respectively protecting peaceful assembly, religious freedom, and notice of charge against state abridgment. Again, the 9-0 *Timbs* decision is too recent to have many confirmations, but Alito gave it credit for incorporating the right against excessive fines.

Table 4: Seven or More Confirmations

Amendment, Right	Relevant Incorporation Case	Clear Confirmations
Fifth, Just Compensation	*Chicago, B & Q Railroad v. Chicago* (1897)	7
Fifth, No Self-Incrimination	*Malloy v. Hogan* (1964)	7
Sixth, Favorable Witnesses	*Washington v. Texas* (1967)	7
Sixth, Public Trial	*In re Oliver* (1948)	8
Fourth, Search and Seizure	*Wolf v. Colorado* (1949)	8
Sixth, Speedy Trial	*Klopfer v. North Carolina* (1967)	8
Sixth, Jury Trial	*Duncan v. Louisiana* (1968)	9
Sixth, Legal Counsel	*Gideon v. Wainwright* (1963)	10
Sixth, Confronting Witnesses	*Pointer v. Texas* (1965)	11
Fifth, No Double Jeopardy	*Benton v. Maryland* (1969)	14

A surprise of this research is just how rarely the Court clearly recognizes incorporation cases, even those that it seems to favor more than others. It may be telling that the Court has confirmed its *Hurtado* refusal to incorporate a right at least as often—14 times—as any case in which it protected a federal right against state governments.

This analysis of justices' statements from their written opinions provides an accounting of which Bill of Rights' guarantees the Court has extended to the states, along with the most relevant incorporation case for each one. It is within the Court's power to confirm federal protections that it has already incorporated and, if it heard cases on the matter, apply the few remaining unincorporated rights to the state level.

APPENDIX A

The Bill of Rights[1]

Amendment I

Congress shall make no law respecting an establishment of religion, or prohibiting the free exercise thereof; or abridging the freedom of speech, or of the press; or the right of the people peaceably to assemble, and to petition the Government for a redress of grievances.

Amendment II

A well regulated Militia, being necessary to the security of a free State, the right of the people to keep and bear Arms, shall not be infringed.

1 The text of the U.S. Bill of Rights is from the National Archives, "The Bill of Rights: A Transcription," www.archives.gov/founding-docs/bill-of-rights-transcript. The states ratified ten of twelve proposed amendments on December 15, 1791, and these ten amendments are conventionally known as the Bill of Rights.

Amendment III

No Soldier shall, in time of peace be quartered in any house, without the consent of the Owner, nor in time of war, but in a manner to be prescribed by law.

Amendment IV

The right of the people to be secure in their persons, houses, papers, and effects, against unreasonable searches and seizures, shall not be violated, and no Warrants shall issue, but upon probable cause, supported by Oath or affirmation, and particularly describing the place to be searched, and the persons or things to be seized.

Amendment V

No person shall be held to answer for a capital, or otherwise infamous crime, unless on a presentment or indictment of a Grand Jury, except in cases arising in the land or naval forces, or in the Militia, when in actual service in time of War or public danger; nor shall any person be subject for the same offence to be twice put in jeopardy of life or limb; nor shall be compelled in any criminal case to be a witness against himself, nor be deprived of life, liberty, or property, without due process of law; nor shall private property be taken for public use, without just compensation.

Amendment VI

In all criminal prosecutions, the accused shall enjoy the right to a speedy and public trial, by an impartial jury of the State and district wherein the crime shall have been committed, which district shall have been previously ascertained by law, and to be informed of the nature and cause of the accusation; to be confronted with the witnesses against him; to have compulsory process for obtaining witnesses in his favor, and to have the Assistance of Counsel for his defence.

Amendment VII

In Suits at common law, where the value in controversy shall exceed twenty dollars, the right of trial by jury shall be preserved, and no fact tried by a jury, shall be otherwise re-examined in any Court of the United States, than according to the rules of the common law.

Amendment VIII

Excessive bail shall not be required, nor excessive fines imposed, nor cruel and unusual punishments inflicted.

Amendment IX

The enumeration in the Constitution, of certain rights, shall not be construed to deny or disparage others retained by the people.

Amendment X

The powers not delegated to the United States by the Constitution, nor prohibited by it to the States, are reserved to the States respectively, or to the people.

APPENDIX B

Incorporated Rights and Relevant Cases by Amendment

Amendment, Right	Incorporation Status	Relevant Incorporation Case
First Amendment, No Establishment of Religion	Incorporated	*Everson v. Board of Education* (1947)
First Amendment, Exercise of Religion	Incorporated	*Cantwell v. Connecticut* (1940)
First Amendment, Freedom of Speech	Incorporated	*Gitlow v. New York* (1925)
First Amendment, Freedom of the Press	Incorporated	*Near v. Minnesota* (1931)
First Amendment, Peaceably Assemble	Incorporated	*De Jonge v. Oregon* (1937)
First Amendment, Petition Government	Incorporated	*Edwards v. South Carolina* (1963)
Second Amendment, Keep and Bear Arms	Incorporated	*McDonald v. Chicago* (2010)
Third Amendment, No Quartering of Soldiers in Homes	Not Incorporated	*Engblom v. Carey* (2d Cir. 1982)
Fourth Amendment, No Unreasonable Searches and Seizures	Incorporated	*Wolf v. Colorado* (1949)

Amendment, Right	**Incorporation Status**	**Relevant Incorporation Case**
Fourth Amendment, Valid Search Warrants	Incorporated	*Aguilar v. Texas* (1964)
Fifth Amendment, Grand Jury	Not Incorporated	*Hurtado v. California* (1884)
Fifth Amendment, No Double Jeopardy	Incorporated	*Benton v. Maryland* (1969)
Fifth Amendment, No Self-Incrimination	Incorporated	*Malloy v. Hogan* (1964)
Fifth Amendment, Due Process of Law	Not Incorporated	*Scott v. McNeal* (1894)
Fifth Amendment, Just Compensation	Incorporated	*Chicago, Burlington & Quincy Railroad v. Chicago* (1897)
Sixth Amendment, Speedy Trial	Incorporated	*Klopfer v. North Carolina* (1967)
Sixth Amendment, Public Trial	Incorporated	*In re Oliver* (1948)
Sixth Amendment, Impartial Jury	Incorporated	*Parker v. Gladden* (1966)
Sixth Amendment, Jury Trial	Incorporated	*Duncan v. Louisiana* (1968)
Sixth Amendment, Jury of Same State and District as Crime	Not Incorporated	*Zicarelli v. Gray* (3d Cir. 1976)
Sixth Amendment, Informed of Accusation	Incorporated	*Cole v. Arkansas* (1948)
Sixth Amendment, Confront Opposing Witnesses	Incorporated	*Pointer v. Texas* (1965)
Sixth Amendment, Favorable Witnesses Process	Incorporated	*Washington v. Texas* (1967)
Sixth Amendment, Counsel	Incorporated	*Gideon v. Wainwright* (1963)
Seventh Amendment, Civil Jury Trial	Not Incorporated	*Walker v. Sauvinet* (1876)
Seventh Amendment, No Re-Examination of Facts	Not Incorporated	*Justices v. Murray* (1870)
Eighth Amendment, No Excessive Bail	Incorporated	*Schilb v. Kuebel* (1971)
Eighth Amendment, No Excessive Fines	Incorporated	*Timbs v. Indiana* (2019)
Eighth Amendment, No Cruel and Unusual Punishments	Incorporated	*Robinson v. California* (1962)

APPENDIX C

Incorporated Rights and Relevant Cases by Year

Amendment, Right	Incorporation Status	Relevant Incorporation Case
Seventh Amendment, No Re-Examination of Facts	Not Incorporated	*Justices v. Murray* (1870)
Seventh Amendment, Civil Jury Trial	Not Incorporated	*Walker v. Sauvinet* (1876)
Fifth Amendment, Grand Jury	Not Incorporated	*Hurtado v. California* (1884)
Fifth Amendment, Due Process of Law	Not Incorporated	*Scott v. McNeal* (1894)
Fifth Amendment, Just Compensation	Incorporated	*Chicago, Burlington & Quincy Railroad v. Chicago* (1897)
First Amendment, Freedom of Speech	Incorporated	*Gitlow v. New York* (1925)
First Amendment, Freedom of the Press	Incorporated	*Near v. Minnesota* (1931)
First Amendment, Peaceably Assemble	Incorporated	*De Jonge v. Oregon* (1937)
First Amendment, Exercise of Religion	Incorporated	*Cantwell v. Connecticut* (1940)
First Amendment, No Establishment of Religion	Incorporated	*Everson v. Board of Education* (1947)

Amendment, Right	Incorporation Status	Relevant Incorporation Case
Sixth Amendment, Informed of Accusation	Incorporated	*Cole v. Arkansas* (1948)
Sixth Amendment, Public Trial	Incorporated	*In re Oliver* (1948)
Fourth Amendment, No Unreasonable Searches and Seizures	Incorporated	*Wolf v. Colorado* (1949)
Eighth Amendment, No Cruel and Unusual Punishments	Incorporated	*Robinson v. California* (1962)
First Amendment, Petition Government	Incorporated	*Edwards v. South Carolina* (1963)
Sixth Amendment, Counsel	Incorporated	*Gideon v. Wainwright* (1963)
Fifth Amendment, No Self-Incrimination	Incorporated	*Malloy v. Hogan* (1964)
Fourth Amendment, Valid Search Warrants	Incorporated	*Aguilar v. Texas* (1964)
Sixth Amendment, Confront Opposing Witnesses	Incorporated	*Pointer v. Texas* (1965)
Sixth Amendment, Impartial Jury	Incorporated	*Parker v. Gladden* (1966)
Sixth Amendment, Speedy Trial	Incorporated	*Klopfer v. North Carolina* (1967)
Sixth Amendment, Favorable Witnesses Process	Incorporated	*Washington v. Texas* (1967)
Sixth Amendment, Jury Trial	Incorporated	*Duncan v. Louisiana* (1968)
Fifth Amendment, No Double Jeopardy	Incorporated	*Benton v. Maryland* (1969)
Eighth Amendment, No Excessive Bail	Incorporated	*Schilb v. Kuebel* (1971)
Sixth Amendment, Jury of Same State and District as Crime	Not Incorporated	*Zicarelli v. Gray* (3d Cir. 1976)
Third Amendment, No Quartering of Soldiers in Homes	Not Incorporated	*Engblom v. Carey* (2d Cir. 1982)
Second Amendment, Keep and Bear Arms	Incorporated	*McDonald v. Chicago* (2010)
Eighth Amendment, No Excessive Fines	Incorporated	*Timbs v. Indiana* (2019)

Bibliography

Abraham, Henry J. *Freedom & the Court: Civil Rights & Liberties in the United States.* New York: Oxford University Press, 1967.

Abraham, Henry J., and Barbara A. Perry. *Freedom & the Court: Civil Rights & Liberties in the United States*. 8th ed. Lawrence: University Press of Kansas, 2003.

Amar, Akhil Reed. "The Bill of Rights and the Fourteenth Amendment." *The Yale Law Journal* 101, no. 6 (April 1992), 1193–284.

Amar, Akhil Reed. *The Constitution and Criminal Procedure: First Principles.* New Haven, CT: Yale University Press, 1997.

Amar, Akhil Reed. *The Bill of Rights: Creation and Reconstruction.* New Haven, CT: Yale University Press, 1998.

Ashmore, Anne. *Dates of Supreme Court Decisions and Arguments: United States Reports Volumes 2–107 (1791–1882).* Washington, DC: U.S. Supreme Court Library, 2018. https://www.supremecourt.gov/opinions/datesofdecisions.pdf.

Barron, Jerome A., and C. Thomas Dienes. *Constitutional Law in a Nutshell.* 5th ed. St. Paul: West, 2003.

Bartholomew, Paul C. "The Gitlow Doctrine Down to Date." *American Bar Association Journal* 50, no. 2 (February 1964), 139–41.

Benner, David. *The 14th Amendment and the Incorporation Doctrine.* Minneapolis: Life & Liberty Publishing, 2017.

Berger, Raoul. *The Fourteenth Amendment and the Bill of Rights.* Norman: University of Oklahoma Press, 1989.

Berger, Raoul. *Government by Judiciary: The Transformation of the Fourteenth Amendment*. 2nd ed. Indianapolis: Liberty Fund, 1997.

Bingham, John A. *One Country, One Constitution, and One People: Speech of Hon. John A. Bingham, of Ohio, in the House of Representatives, February 28, 1866, in Support of the Proposed Amendment to Enforce the Bill of Rights*. Washington, DC: Congressional Globe Office, 1866.

Brennan, William J., Jr. "The Bill of Rights and the States." *New York University Law Review* 36, no. 4 (1961), 761–78.

Brennan, William J., Jr. "State Constitutions and the Protection of Individual Rights." *Harvard Law Review* 90, no. 3 (January 1977), 489–504.

Brennan, William J., Jr. "The Bill of Rights and the States: The Revival of State Constitutions as Guardians of Individual Rights." *New York University Law Review* 6, no. 4 (October 1986), 535–53.

Brown, Rebecca L. "Separated Powers and Ordered Liberty." *University of Pennsylvania Law Review* 139, no. 6 (June 1991), 1513–66.

Carp, Robert A., Kenneth L. Manning, and Lisa M. Holmes, *Judicial Process in America*. 12th ed. Washington, DC: CQ Press, 2022.

Cortner, Richard C. *The Supreme Court and the Second Bill of Rights: The Fourteenth Amendment and the Nationalization of Civil Liberties*. Madison: University of Wisconsin Press, 1981.

Currie, David P. "The Constitution in the Supreme Court: Full Faith and the Bill of Rights, 1889–1910." *The University of Chicago Law Review* 52, no. 4 (Autumn 1985), 867–902.

Currie, David P. "The Constitution in the Supreme Court: Civil Rights and Liberties, 1930–1941." *Duke Law Journal* 1987, no. 5 (November 1987), 800–30.

Currie, David P. *The Constitution in the Supreme Court: The Second Century,* 1888–1986. Chicago: University of Chicago Press, 1994.

Curtis, Michael Kent. *No State Shall Abridge: The Fourteenth Amendment and the Bill of Rights*. Durham, NC: Duke University Press, 1986.

Dressler, Joshua, and Alan C. Michaels. *Understanding Criminal Procedure: Volume 2, Adjudication*. 4th ed. Durham, NC: Carolina Academic Press, 2015.

Dressler, Joshua, Alan C. Michaels, and Ric Simmons. *Understanding Criminal Procedure: Volume 1, Investigation*. 8th ed. Durham, NC: Carolina Academic Press, 2021.

Dworkin, Ronald. "Unenumerated Rights: Whether and How *Roe* should be Overruled." *The University of Chicago Law Review* 59, no. 1 (Winter 1992), 381–432.

Epps, Garrett. *Democracy Reborn: The Fourteenth Amendment and the Fight for Equal Rights in Post-Civil War America*. New York: Henry Holt, 2006.

Epps, Garrett. *American Epic: Reading the U.S. Constitution*. Oxford: Oxford University Press, 2013.

Epstein, Lee, Kevin T. McGuire, and Thomas G. Walker. *Constitutional Law for a Changing America: Rights, Liberties, and Justice*. 11th ed. Washington, DC: CQ Press, 2021.

Excellence in First Amendment Studies. *The First Amendment Encyclopedia*. Murfreesboro: Middle Tennessee State and Washington, DC: Sage, 2016, https://www.mtsu.edu/first-amendment/encyclopedia.

Fairman, Charles. "Does the Fourteenth Amendment Incorporate the Bill of Rights? The Original Understanding." *Stanford Law Review* 2, no. 1 (December 1949), 140–73.

Fairman, Charles, Leonard Levy, and Stanley Morrison. *Introduction to the Fourteenth Amendment and the Bill of Rights: The Incorporation Theory*. New York: De Capo, 1970.

Fallon, Richard H., Jr. *The Dynamic Constitution: An Introduction to American Constitutional Law*. New York: Cambridge University Press, 2004.

Fallon, Richard H., Jr. *The Nature of Constitutional Rights: The Invention and Logic of Strict Judicial Scrutiny*. New York: Cambridge University Press, 2019.

Finkelman, Paul, ed. *Encyclopedia of American Civil Liberties*. 3 vols. New York: Routledge, 2021.

Fisher, Louis, and Katy J. Harriger. *American Constitutional Law*. 12th ed. Durham, NC: Carolina Academic Press, 2019.

Flack, Horace. *The Adoption of the Fourteenth Amendment*. Baltimore, MD: Johns Hopkins University Press, 1908.

Frankfurter, Felix. "Memorandum on 'Incorporation' of the Bill of Rights into the Due Process Clause of the Fourteenth Amendment." *Harvard Law Review* 78, no. 4 (February 1965): 746–83.

Friendly, Fred W., and Martha J. H. Elliot. *The Constitution That Delicate Balance: Landmark Cases that Shaped the Constitution*. New York: McGraw-Hill, 1984.

Gillman, Howard. "Preferred Freedoms: The Progressive Expansion of State Power and the Rise of Modern Civil Liberties Jurisprudence." *Political Research Quarterly* 47, no. 3 (September 1994), 623–53.

Glidden, William B. *Congress and the Fourteenth Amendment: Enforcing Liberty and Equality in the States*. Lanham, MD: Lexington Books, 2013.

Gunn, T. Jeremy, and John Witte Jr., eds. *No Establishment of Religion: America's Original Contribution to Religious Liberty*. New York: Oxford University Press, 2012.

Henkin, Louis. "Selective Incorporation in the Fourteenth Amendment." *Yale Law Journal* 73, no. 1 (November 1963), 74–88.

Hudson, David L., David A. Schultz, and John R. Vile, eds. *The Encyclopedia of the First Amendment*. Washington, DC: CQ Press, 2009.

Israel, Jerold H. "Selective Incorporation: Revisited." *Georgetown Law Journal* 71, no. 2 (December 1982), 253–338.

Kafker, Scott. "The Right to Venue and the Right to an Impartial Jury: Resolving the Conflict in the Federal Constitution." *The University of Chicago Law Review* 52, no. 3 (Summer 1985), 729–50.

Klarman, Michael J. "Rethinking the Civil Rights and Civil Liberties Revolution." *Virginia Law Review* 82, no. 1 (February 1996), 1–67.

Lash, Kurt T. "Respeaking the Bill of Rights: A New Doctrine of Incorporation." *Indiana Law Journal* 97, no. 4 (January 15, 2021), 1439–53.

Lehman, Jeffrey, and Shirell Phelps. *West's Encyclopedia of American* Law, 2nd ed. Detroit: Thomson/Gale, 2005.

Lewis, Thomas T., ed. *The Bill of Rights, Volume* 1*: The Bill of Rights, The Amendments, The Issues.* Pasadena, CA: Salem Press, 2002.

Library of Congress. "United States Reports (Official Opinions of the U.S. Supreme Court)." *Digital Collections.* https://www.loc.gov/collections/united-states-reports/.

Marietta, Morgan. *A Citizen's Guide to the Constitution and the Supreme Court.* New York: Routledge, 2014.

Mason, Alpheus Thomas. "The Core of Free Government, 1938–40: Mr. Justice Stone and 'Preferred Freedoms.'" *The Yale Law Journal* 65, no. 5 (April 1956), 597–628.

Mathias, Charles M., Jr. "Ordered Liberty: The Original Intent of the Constitution." *Maryland Law Review* 47, no. 1 (1987), 174–88.

McCloskey, Robert G. "Economic Due Process and the Supreme Court: An Exhumation and Reburial." *The Supreme Court Review* 1962 (1962), 34–62.

Morrison, Stanley. "Does the Fourteenth Amendment Incorporate the Bill of Rights? The Judicial Interpretation." *Stanford Law Review* 2, no. 1 (December 1949), 140–73.

Murphy, Paul L., ed. *Pre-Nineteen Sixty Developments in the Bill of Rights Area.* 2 vols. 3rd ed. New York: Routledge, 2013.

Mykkeltvedt, Roald Y. *Nationalization of the Bill of Rights: Fourteenth Amendment Due Process and Procedural Rights.* Port Washington, NY: National University Publications, 1983.

National Archives. "The Bill of Rights: A Transcription." www.archives.gov/founding-docs/bill-of-rights-transcript.

Nourse, Victoria F. "A Tale of Two Lochners: The Untold History of Substantive Due Process and the Idea of Fundamental Rights." *California Law Review* 97, no. 3 (June 2009), 751–99.

O'Brien, David M., and Gordon Silverstein. *Constitutional Law and Politics: Volume 2, Civil Rights and Civil Liberties.* 11th ed. New York: W.W. Norton, 2020.

Powe, Lucas A., Jr. *The Warren Court and American Politics.* Cambridge, MA: Harvard University Press, 2002.

Primus, Richard A. *The American Language of Rights.* New York: Cambridge University Press, 1999.

Rosenthal, Lawrence. "The New Originalism Meets the Fourteenth Amendment: Original Public Meaning and the Problem of Incorporation." *Journal of Contemporary Legal Issues* 18 (2009), 361–408.

Rubin, Peter J. "Square Pegs and Round Holes: Substantive Due Process, Procedural Due Process, and the Bill of Rights." *Columbia Law Review* 103, no. 4 (May 2003), 833–92.

Schopler, Ernest H. "Comment Note—What Provisions of the Federal Constitution's Bill of Rights are Applicable to the States?" (23 L. Ed. 2d 985).

Supreme Court. "Opinions: U.S. Reports." https://www.supremecourt.gov/opinions/USReports.aspx.

Supreme Court. "Justices 1789 to Present." http://www.supremecourt.gov/about/members_text.aspx.

Thomas, Suja A. "Nonincorporation: The Bill of Rights after McDonald v. Chicago." *Notre Dame Law Review* 88, no. 1 (November 2012), 159–318.

Vile, John R. *A Companion to the United States Constitution and Its Amendments*. 7th ed. Santa Barbara, CA: Praeger 2021.

Vile, John R., and David Schultz. *Encyclopedia of Civil Liberties in America*. 3 vols. London: Routledge, 2015.

Walker, Frank. "Constitutional Law—Was it Intended that the Fourteenth Amendment Incorporate the Bill of Rights?" *North Carolina Law Review* 42, no. 4 (1964), 925–36.

Wermiel, Stephen J. "Rights in the Modern Era: Applying the Bill of Rights to the States." *William & Mary Bill of Rights Journal* 1, no. 1 (May 1992), 121–30.

Wildenthal, Bryan. "Nationalizing the Bill of Rights: Revisiting the Original Understanding of the Fourteenth Amendment in 1866–67." *Ohio State Law Journal* 68, no. 6 (2007), 1509–58.

Cases

Index

www.ingramcontent.com/pod-product-compliance
Ingram Content Group UK Ltd.
Pitfield, Milton Keynes, MK11 3LW, UK
UKHW020840290926
15470UKWH00004B/1469

9 781433 196317